Sweets and Candies

HAMLYN COOKSHELF SERIES

Sweets and Candies

Marguerite Patten

HAMLYN

London · New York · Sydney · Toronto

The following titles are also available in this series:

Cooking with Yogurt · The Food Processor Cookbook
Mighty Mince Cookbook · Potato Cookery

Front cover photograph by James Jackson
Photography by Martin Brigdale

Line drawings by Roberta Colegate-Stone

Published in 1984 by
The Hamlyn Publishing Group Limited
London · New York · Sydney · Toronto
Astronaut House, Feltham, Middlesex, England

This material was originally published as *500 Recipes for Sweets
and Candies*

© Copyright The Hamlyn Publishing Group Limited 1964,
1984

ISBN 0 600 32408 7 (hardback)
0 600 32420 6 (softback)

Set in Monophoto Garamond
by Tameside Filmsetting Limited, Lancashire

Printed in Yugoslavia

Contents

Useful Facts and Figures

Notes on metrication

In this book quantities are given in metric and Imperial measures. Exact conversion from Imperial to metric measures does not usually give very convenient working quantities and so the metric measures have been rounded off into units of 25 grams. The table below shows the recommended equivalents.

Ounces	Approx g to nearest whole figure	Recommended conversion to nearest unit of 25
1	28	25
2	57	50
3	85	75
4	113	100
5	142	150
6	170	175
7	198	200
8	227	225
9	255	250
10	283	275
11	312	300
12	340	350
13	368	375
14	396	400
15	425	425
16 (1 lb)	454	450

Note: When converting quantities over 16 oz first add the appropriate figures in the centre column, then adjust to the nearest unit of 25. As a general guide, 1 kg (1000 g) equals 2.2 lb or about 2 lb 3 oz. This method of conversion gives good results in nearly all cases, although in certain pastry and cake recipes a more accurate conversion is necessary to produce a balanced recipe.

Liquid measures The millilitre has been used in this book and the following table gives a few examples.

Imperial	Approx ml to nearest whole figure	Recommended ml
$\frac{1}{4}$ pint	142	150 ml
$\frac{1}{2}$ pint	283	300 ml
$\frac{3}{4}$ pint	425	450 ml
1 pint	567	600 ml
$1\frac{1}{2}$ pints	851	900 ml
$1\frac{3}{4}$ pints	992	1000 ml (1 litre)

Spoon measures All spoon measures given in this book are level unless otherwise stated.

Can sizes At present, cans are marked with the exact (usually to the nearest whole number) metric equivalent of the Imperial weight of the contents, so we have followed this practice when giving can sizes.

Oven temperatures The table below gives recommended equivalents.

	°C	°F	Gas Mark
Very cool	110	225	$\frac{1}{4}$
	120	250	$\frac{1}{2}$
Cool	140	275	1
	150	300	2
Moderate	160	325	3
	180	350	4
Moderately hot	190	375	5
	200	400	6
Hot	220	425	7
	230	450	8
Very hot	240	475	9

Notes for American and Australian users

In America the 8-fl oz measuring cup is used. In Australia metric measures are now used in conjunction with the standard 250-ml measuring cup. The Imperial pint, used in Britain and Australia, is 20 fl oz, while the American pint is 16 fl oz. It is important to remember that the Australian tablespoon differs from both the British and American tablespoons; the table below gives a comparison. The British standard tablespoon, which has been used throughout this book, holds 17.7 ml, the American 14.2 ml, and the Australian 20 ml. A teaspoon holds approximately 5 ml in all three countries.

British	American	Australian
1 teaspoon	1 teaspoon	1 teaspoon
1 tablespoon	1 tablespoon	1 tablespoon
2 tablespoons	3 tablespoons	2 tablespoons
$3\frac{1}{2}$ tablespoons	4 tablespoons	3 tablespoons
4 tablespoons	5 tablespoons	$3\frac{1}{2}$ tablespoons

An Imperial/American guide to solid and liquid measures

SOLID MEASURES

Imperial	American
1 lb butter or margarine	2 cups
1 lb flour	4 cups
1 lb granulated or caster sugar	2 cups
1 lb icing sugar	3 cups
8 oz rice	1 cup

LIQUID MEASURES

Imperial	American
$\frac{1}{4}$ pint liquid	$\frac{2}{3}$ cup liquid
$\frac{1}{2}$ pint	$1\frac{1}{4}$ cups
$\frac{3}{4}$ pint	2 cups
1 pint	$2\frac{1}{2}$ cups
$1\frac{1}{2}$ pints	$3\frac{3}{4}$ cups
2 pints	5 cups ($2\frac{1}{2}$ pints)

Note: When making any of the recipes in this book, only follow one set of measures as they are not interchangeable.

Introduction

To many people sweet-making is an unknown form of cooking, but I am confident that once you start you will find it a most enjoyable and rewarding hobby. It can prove quite economical since many sweets are relatively inexpensive to make, and this book gives a wide range of recipes that are satisfactory to prepare at home. Homemade chocolate is not included since this requires professional skill and the right conditions; there are however ideas for coating fillings and other sweetmeats with chocolate, which can be an outstanding success. I hope that beginners and children will be encouraged to start making confectionery by trying the selection of uncooked sweetmeats given throughout the book.

It is important to follow the basic rules for sweet-making, in particular when the mixture is being cooked at, or must reach, a very high temperature, because you will spoil the mixture by under or over-boiling. The information on the following pages, and at the beginning of each section, will help you to avoid disappointment. If you intend to make a lot of sweets it is well worthwhile investing in a sugar thermometer because this does lessen the chance of inaccuracy. On page 11 details are given of the specialist equipment required for sweet making.

You will find that homemade sweets are always a great success at charity fêtes and bazaars, as well as making popular family presents.

In addition to the variety of sweetmeats in this book, you will find a selection of petits-fours. These will be appreciated when you are planning a special dinner or luncheon party or they can be served with tea or coffee. A number of the recipes are suitable for long-term storage or freezing.

Sweet-making is something that gives me great pleasure. I hope you will be equally delighted with the results you produce.

MARGUERITE PATTEN

Nine Points for Successful Sweet-Making

1. Choose a strong saucepan, for you will be heating the ingredients to a very high temperature and they are likely to burn if a thin pan, or one with an uneven base, is used.

2. As well as a strong pan, do choose a sufficiently large one. The mixture is likely to rise as it boils and could boil over.

3. Keep a bowl of cold water and a pastry brush beside you. This is to brush down the inside of the pan occasionally as the sugar mixture bubbles up during cooking, to prevent the mixture hardening on the sides of the pan and forming crystals.

4. Stir as little as possible. In some recipes, like fudge, where you have a high percentage of milk or cream, you will need to stir from time to time to prevent burning. Continual stirring does slow up the cooking of the mixture and can prevent it reaching the right temperature; it also encourages crystallization.

5. In spite of the comments in point 4, it is vital to stir until all the sugar in the mixture is dissolved thoroughly. If you do not do this, there is a possibility that the dry sugar will crystallize and burn at the bottom of the pan.

6. To make homemade sweets which entail cooking is not as easy as many people suppose because you are boiling the ingredients to a temperature which must be correct if you are to have the desired result. As in jam making, your sweets will be spoiled if they are either over or under-boiled. Some people have had very unexpected results when trying to make fudge; for example, by boiling the fudge mixture to too high a temperature they have ended up with toffee!

7. Unless you have a sugar thermometer, start testing after just a few minutes, so that you are sure the mixture is not overcooked. It is almost impossible to give a definite boiling time for most sweetmeats without seeing the exact heat available and the size of pan. The wider the diameter of a pan, the shorter the cooking time.

8. ALWAYS REMOVE THE PAN FROM THE HEAT WHILE YOU TEST so the mixture does not continue to cook.

9. When the tins for the cooked mixture have to be greased use butter, margarine or oil; allow the sweets to cool at room temperature unless stated to the contrary.

Equipment for Sweet-Making

Strong saucepan(s) (see points 1 and 2, opposite): a good heavy aluminium pan is excellent.

Firm wooden spoons: choose those with long handles so your hands are well away from the hot sugar when stirring.

A pastry brush (see point 3, opposite): buy a good quality brush that will withstand heat.

A sugar thermometer: almost an essential if you are going to do a lot of sweet-making, as it enables you to tell the temperature without any guesswork; it is also a great asset when making preserves.

A marble slab (for working the sweetmeats): these are not easy to obtain today and the cheapest way of getting one is through a second-hand dealer, who may be able to sell you a marble slab from an old dressing table. You can, however, buy a slab from a firm which specializes in high-class cookery and sweet-making equipment. A laminated board could be used instead.

Moulds: these take various forms. Fondant sweets are put into rubber moulds and you buy sets of these. Metal moulds can be used as well, providing you can get them in a sufficiently small size.

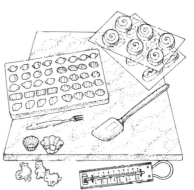

A dipping fork: for coating sweets in melted chocolate or fondant you need a very fine fork. A fine skewer could be used as a substitute.

Kitchen scissors: these are useful for cutting certain sweets.

A small hammer: for breaking very hard, brittle toffee. A good ironmonger will sell one.

A funnel: this will assist when filling tiny moulds with the very hot liquid sugar mixture.

A scraper: although an ordinary palette knife can be used to pick up the sugar mixture from a marble slab when moulding, a more pliable scraper or spatula is easier to handle.

Tins (for the cooked mixture): ordinary aluminium tins with a flat base can be used for the sweet mixture.

Care of Equipment

Saucepan: this can be difficult to clean after sweet-making unless you fill the pan with cold water, heat this gently until the sugar mixture has melted again, then wash the pan as usual.

Pastry brush: wash the bristles in plenty of hot water to melt any sugar mixture on the brush, rinse in cold water and allow to drain. Dry thoroughly before putting away.

Sugar thermometer: never take the thermometer from the great heat of the sugar mixture in the pan and put it on to a cold surface. Stand on a wooden board until it is quite cool. Wash gently in warm water to remove the sticky sugar mixture, dry thoroughly and store in a safe place.

Wooden spoons, spatulas: wash as soon as possible after use so that the sweet mixture does not have a chance to set. Use moderately warm washing-up water, rinse and dry thoroughly before putting away.

Tins: it should be easy to remove the cold sweets and, therefore, not difficult to clean the tin. Wash in the usual way and dry thoroughly before storing.

Moulds: metal moulds are treated just like metal tins but rubber moulds should never be cleaned in very hot water; use lukewarm water, dry well. Store rubber moulds in a dry cupboard that is well ventilated but not too hot.

Storing Completed Sweetmeats

In order to keep sweetmeats in prime condition allow the cooked mixture to cool completely in the moulds, tin or tray and then pack in an airtight tin or box or other container. Advice on attractive containers is given in Chapter 7, which begins on page 124. In some cases the sweetmeats must be individually wrapped to prevent their becoming over-sticky or over-soft with storage. Choose waxed, rather than greaseproof, paper. It is more pliable and encloses the sweetmeats better.

Heat for Cooking Sugar Mixtures

At all times the heat under the saucepan in which the sugar mixture is cooked is very important. The method in the recipes mentions the exact heat, where this is important.

In many recipes the words 'low heat' are used. This is because the mixture is an exceptionally rich one, containing full-cream canned milk, or cream, and butter as well as the sugar and this is very inclined to burn. In other recipes a less specific term is used, which means that you can have a moderate heat. There is no virtue in cooking sweets very slowly unless specifically recommended, for this hinders the mixture reaching the right stage.

When using a gas cooker check carefully that the flames are not coming up the sides of the pan; this would cause the mixture to over-cook on the inside of the saucepan.

To Make Sweets Safely

1. Keep members of the family, and small children in particular, away from the cooker when you are boiling sweets, for a burn from a sugar mixture, especially when it has reached a very high temperature, could be very serious indeed.

2. Never allow children to make boiled sweets without adult supervision.

3. Check that the pan on the cooker is carefully balanced and the handle turned inwards towards the cooker so that no-one will catch their hand or arm on the handle. If the pan tipped over, the very high temperature of the contents could cause a serious fire and accident.

4. Put everything for testing near to the pan; even drips of the extremely hot sugar mixture would burn the skin.

5. If the recipe states that the cooking utensil should be put into cold water for rapid cooling, make sure the container used for the water is unbreakable (for example a stainless steel sink) as the saucepan will be extremely hot. Most plastics are likely to lose their shape when in contact with hot metal.

Ingredients for Sweet-Making

Use the best quality ingredients available, weigh or measure accurately. The most important ingredients in sweet-making are:

BUTTER, MARGARINE OR OIL

Choose unsalted butter; margarine can be substituted in some recipes and this is indicated in the list of ingredients. If brushing a tin with butter or margarine this should be melted and used sparingly; if using oil for this purpose choose very good quality olive or corn oil.

COLOURING

In some recipes colouring is used. Choose delicate culinary colourings and add sparingly from a skewer, as described under flavouring below.

FLAVOURING

This is provided in various ways, for example by adding fruit and nuts as described below. Essences can also be used to flavour the mixture. Use these carefully, they are very strong. If only a few drops are required put a skewer in the bottle and allow the drops adhering to the skewer to drop into the mixture.

Alcohol is delicious in certain sweetmeats, such as in fudge, see page 18. Liqueurs are particularly suitable because they have a sweet and concentrated flavouring.

FRUIT

Dried fruit is an important ingredient in many sweetmeats. If the fruit seems a little dry, take the liquid from the recipe, put it into a bowl with the fruit and allow to stand for 1-2 hours. Strain the liquid (do not increase the amount) and use in the recipe.

Fresh fruit juices are sometimes used, also the rinds of citrus fruits. Grate the rind very finely and use only the top part (the 'zest').

MILK AND CREAM

If using fresh milk use the creamiest kind possible. Choose the type of cream recommended in the recipe. Canned milk is used in many sweetmeats; buy full-cream condensed (sweetened) or full-cream evaporated (unsweetened) milk. Use the undiluted milk from the can.

NUTS

Many nuts are used in sweet-making. In most cases these must be 'blanched', i.e. skinned. Almonds can be obtained ready-blanched, but if obtained in their skins, put the nuts into boiling water, leave for 30-60 seconds, remove and skin. Pistachio nuts are skinned in the same way. Brazils and other nuts have skins that are less easy to remove; put these nuts into a moderately hot oven (190 c, 375 f, gas 5) for 4-5 minutes, cool slightly then rub away the skins.

SUGAR

Granulated sugar is ideal for many sweetmeats. Castor or loaf sugar can be substituted, but these are more expensive than granulated and have no advantage in most sweetmeats. When brown sugar is required, the ideal choice is demerara, as the flavour is not too strong. The best alternative, if demerara is not available, is moist light brown sugar. A rich dark sugar, such as Barbados, will change the colour and flavour.

SYRUP AND TREACLE

Golden syrup gives a sweet and pleasantly mild flavour to a mixture. If you substitute black treacle (molasses) the sweetmeat will have an entirely different appearance and taste.

To weigh syrup or treacle, weigh the empty saucepan, or the saucepan containing the first ingredients required in the recipe. Place a weight on the scales to cover the required amount of syrup or treacle, then gradually spoon the right quantity into the saucepan.

If you would prefer to measure, rather than weigh, the syrup or treacle, a standard tablespoon weighs 25 g/1 oz.

MISCELLANEOUS

Cream of tartar, tartaric acid and glucose help to avoid crystallization, see also points 3-5 on page 10. Glucose also imparts a sweetness to the mixture. Unless specifically stated use either powdered or liquid glucose. Liquid glucose adds a glossy appearance to the sweets and makes the mixture more pliable and therefore easier to handle.

Stages of Sugar Boiling

Have a basin or cup of cold water available and drop in a small quantity of the mixture to see which stage has been reached.

WITH A SUGAR THERMOMETER

Allow the mixture to boil in the pan for a minute or two after the sugar has thoroughly dissolved. Put in the thermometer and gently move this around in the mixture. This gives you an overall and accurate reading. Try to read the thermometer quickly and without lifting it too far out of the sugar mixture, for the temperature drops rapidly when the thermometer is removed.

Whether you are testing with or without a thermometer, remove the pan from the heat as you test or take the reading, and do not replace on the heat unless you are satisfied further cooking is necessary.

TEMPERATURES AND APPEARANCE

Description	Temperature °C	°F	Appearance
Thread	107.2 to 108.8	225 to 228	The syrup is so thin that it runs off the spoon into the cold water. If kept on the spoon for a moment and pinched, it forms a hot substance. A stage rarely used in sweet-making except as a sticking coating. For a firmer coating boil to 108.8 c/228 f.
Pearl	110 to 111.6	230 to 233	The syrup forms tiny pearl-like balls in the cold water, too soft to form a sweetmeat. This stage is used occasionally for binding or coating ingredients.
Blow	112.7	235	The bubbles float when tested in cold water. A continuation of the pearl stage, not a sweetmeat stage.

Soft Ball	114.4 to 115.5	238 to 240	When the sweet mixture drops into the cold water it can be gathered up and formed into a soft ball with the fingers. Used for fudge and other sweetmeats; fondant mixtures are boiled to a slightly higher temperature.
Firm Ball	118.3 to 121.1	245 to 250	The sugar mixture can be formed into a pliable, but firmer ball at this temperature. Used for caramels. A firmer ball (or 'light crack') is made by increasing the temperatures up to 126.6-132.2c/260-270 f. Between 132.2-138 c/270-280 f, there is a stage which has no particular characteristics.
Crack	138 to 143.3	280 to 290	In the crack stage the sugar mixture will break quite easily between your fingers. This temperature is used for certain toffees or sweets like butterscotch; the crack stage continues up to the next stage, the higher the temperature the more brittle the mixture.
Caramel	155.5 to 177	312 to 350	At this stage the sugar mixture begins to change colour drastically; it caramelizes – not to be confused with caramels. Care must be taken not to exceed this for if the sugar mixture boils above this stage it becomes over-brown, then blackens. Too dark a caramel tastes bitter and unpalatable; any temperature above 177c/350f makes the caramel too dark.

CHAPTER I

SOFT AND CREAMY

Fudge, candy and nougat are some of the most successful sweetmeats to make at home. Their success depends upon using rather rich ingredients, such as butter and cream, or full-cream canned milk. Often less high-class ingredients are used in the commercial versions of these sweetmeats in order to reduce the cost.

Fudge and candy are rather similar but the texture is different. Fudge must be smooth, creamy and opaque (caused by beating the hot mixture); whereas candy, while having a creamy taste, is crisp, crumbly and clearer in appearance (the mixture is not beaten like fudge). The golden rules for making perfect fudge follow on this and the next page and those for making candy on page 33.

Nougat is an exotic sweetmeat that comes from the Middle East and France. Good nougat should not be too hard; it can seem slightly hard as you begin to eat it, then it should soften and become deliciously creamy, a perfect contrast to the firmness of the nuts it contains. The information on making nougat is on page 38. This is a less simple sweetmeat than many others, for in most nougat recipes you have to deal with the sugar mixture – the honey – and the egg whites. It means working quite strictly in the order given in the recipe, so that all ingredients are ready at the right time.

Fudge

Fudge is a soft creamy sweetmeat that is a favourite with most people because it is easy to eat and has a delicious flavour. Unless you are preparing fudge for a special occasion such as a 'bring and buy' sale, it is better to make the sweetmeat in relatively small amounts, as in the recipes, so the mixture can be stirred and beaten efficiently in the saucepan.

METHOD OF MAKING FUDGE

The recipes for making fudge vary in the proportions used, but the mixture should contain butter as well as milk and/or cream or full-cream evaporated (unsweetened) canned milk or full-cream condensed (sweetened) canned milk.

USE OF FUDGE

Fudge is a sweetmeat by itself; it can be covered in chocolate but it is too sweet to be coated with fondant. A variety of ingredients (nuts, dried fruit, etc.) can be added.

DISADVANTAGES OF FUDGE

Fudge is very high in calories, it is also eaten very quickly and cannot therefore be described as an economical sweet to make for home purposes. It becomes rather hard and loses its creaminess with prolonged storage.

PROBLEMS OF MAKING FUDGE

Because of the high cream or milk content, fudge has a tendency to burn in the pan and it must be stirred from time to time; the nearer the mixture gets to the 'soft ball' stage, the more it is inclined to stick to the pan and the more it should be stirred.

You must heat fudge until it turns slightly cloudy in the pan, otherwise it may well become granular (sugary).

Although you must boil to the correct temperature given in the recipes, take care *not to exceed this*, otherwise you will lose the soft creamy texture of the fudge. Although 114.4 c/238 f is the average temperature for fudge to set, if you are making the fudge in very hot weather, boil to 115.5 c/240 f, to be sure it will set in the greater heat.

You must be sure to reach the temperatures given in the recipes.

TO STORE FUDGE

Store away from excess heat or dampness otherwise the fudge will become sticky-looking on the outside. Keep in an airtight container to prevent it hardening and losing its soft texture.

TO REHEAT FUDGE

Fudge is never as good if kept for very long periods, so it is inadvisable to reheat the sweetmeat.

Vanilla Fudge 1

Economical recipe.

450 g/1 lb granulated sugar
300 ml/$\frac{1}{2}$ pint milk
50 g/2 oz butter or margarine
$\frac{1}{2}$-1 teaspoon vanilla essence

Put the ingredients into a strong saucepan. Stir over a low heat until the sugar has dissolved. Boil steadily, stirring only occasionally (to prevent the mixture burning), until the fudge reaches 'soft ball' stage or 114 c/238 f. Remove the pan from the heat and beat until the mixture just *begins* to thicken and becomes opaque (cloudy) in appearance. This is very important when making fudge.

Grease a 20-cm/8-in square sandwich tin with a little melted butter or oil. Pour in the fudge and leave until almost set; cut into neat pieces with a sharp knife. Leave in the tin until quite firm. Fudge does not need wrapping in waxed paper, although this can be done if preferred.

Note This recipe produces the type of fudge that is pleasant to eat, but which lacks the creamy texture of many richer recipes. These will be found on pages 26–29. This fudge tends to harden slightly with prolonged storage and becomes almost like a candy.

Vanilla Fudge 2

A creamy sweetmeat.

450 g/1 lb granulated sugar
1 (397-g/14-oz) can full-cream condensed (sweetened) milk
50 g/2 oz butter or margarine
150 ml/$\frac{1}{4}$ pint water
$\frac{1}{2}$-1 teaspoon vanilla essence

Put all the ingredients into a strong saucepan. Stir over a low heat until the sugar has dissolved. Continue as Vanilla Fudge 1, above.

VARIATIONS ON VANILLA FUDGE

The following flavours are based on the recipes for Vanilla Fudge, recipes 1 or 2, using 450 g/1 lb sugar (see left).

Almond Fudge: use almond instead of vanilla essence. Chop 50 g/2 oz blanched almonds, add to the fudge when setting point is nearly reached.

Cherry Fudge: use the vanilla essence as in the recipe. Chop 50-100 g/2-4 oz glacé cherries; add these when setting point is nearly reached.

Chocolate Fudge: blend 2 tablespoons cocoa powder or 4 tablespoons chocolate powder or 75-100 g/3-4 oz chopped plain chocolate into the mixture when the sugar has melted.

Coffee Fudge: use 150 ml/¼ pint strong black coffee and 150 ml/¼ pint milk instead of 300 ml/½ pint milk in recipe 1, or 150 ml/¼ pint strong black coffee instead of 150 ml/¼ pint water in recipe 2.

Fruit Fudge: add approximately 100 g/4 oz mixed dried fruit just before setting point is reached.

Ginger Fudge: omit the vanilla essence. Chop 50-100 g/2-4 oz crystallized or well-drained preserved ginger. Add this with 1 teaspoon ground ginger to the fudge just before setting point is reached.

Honey Fudge: use 350 g/12 oz sugar and 100 g/4 oz honey in the recipe in place of 450 g/1 lb sugar.

Lemon Fudge: omit the vanilla essence. Add the finely grated rind of 1-2 lemons with the sugar. Chop 50-100 g/2-4 oz candied lemon peel and add to the fudge just before setting point is reached.

Nut Fudge: any nuts can be added to fudge, using 50-175 g/2-6 oz. These should be skinned where possible, chopped and added just before setting point is reached.

Orange Fudge: omit the vanilla essence. Add the finely grated rind of 2 oranges with 50-100 g/2-4 oz chopped candied orange peel; add to the fudge just before setting point is reached.

Peanut Fudge: shell the peanuts by heating in the oven for a few minutes, then rubbing off the skins. Chop and add 50-175 g/2-6 oz just before setting point is reached.

Raisin Fudge: Add approximately 100 g/4 oz raisins just before setting point is reached.

Sultana Fudge: Add approximately 100 g/4 oz sultanas just before setting point is reached.

Treacle Fudge: Use 350 g/12 oz sugar and 100 g/4 oz black treacle instead of 450 g/1 lb sugar. Do not exceed this proportion of treacle.

Banana Fudge

3 tablespoons water
50 g/2 oz butter
1 (410-g/14½-oz) can full-cream evaporated (unsweetened) milk
450 g/1 lb granulated sugar
2 large or 3 small ripe bananas
grated rind of 1 lemon

Put the water, butter, evaporated milk and sugar into a strong saucepan. Stir over a low heat until the sugar dissolves then allow the mixture to boil for 2-3 minutes.

Peel and mash the bananas with the lemon rind, add to the sugar mixture then continue as Vanilla Fudge 1, page 20.

Note Do not peel and mash the bananas until ready to add to the sugar mixture.

Chiffon Fudge

A light coloured and delicate fudge.

450 g/1 lb castor sugar or icing sugar, sifted
150 ml/¼ pint milk
150 ml/¼ pint double cream
25 g/1 oz butter
½ teaspoon vanilla essence

Put all the ingredients into a strong saucepan. Stir over a low heat until the sugar has dissolved, then continue as Vanilla Fudge 1, page 20.

VARIATIONS

Almond Chiffon Fudge: use ½ teaspoon almond essence instead of vanilla and add 75 g/3 oz finely chopped blanched almonds.

Coconut Chiffon Fudge: add 100 g/4 oz desiccated coconut just before the 'soft ball' stage is reached.

Raisin Chiffon Fudge: add 100 g/4 oz seedless raisins just before the 'soft ball' stage is reached.

Sultana Chiffon Fudge: add 100 g/4 oz light coloured sultanas just before the 'soft ball' stage is reached.

Butter Fudge

50 g/2 oz butter
4 tablespoons water
2 tablespoons golden syrup
450 g/1 lb granulated sugar
8 tablespoons full-cream condensed (sweetened) canned milk

Put all the ingredients into a strong saucepan; stir over a low heat until the sugar dissolves then continue as Vanilla Fudge 1, page 20.

Note This fudge can be used as the basis of Fruit Fudge (page 21) or Raisin or Sultana Fudge, (opposite).

Brown Sugar Fudge

Make any of the fudge recipes using half white, half brown (demerara) sugar. In the richer recipes, all brown sugar has a tendency to make the mixture curdle. Natural granulated sugar, which is pale golden in colour, gives a good flavour and colour.

Maple Fudge

Use any of the fudge recipes on pages 20 to top of 22, but use half sugar and half maple syrup in place of all sugar.

VARIATION

Peanut Fudge: use any of the fudge recipes in this book but substitute peanut butter for butter in the recipes, or use half butter and half peanut butter, and add 100-175 g/4-6 oz skinned peanuts to the mixture just before the 'soft ball' stage is reached.

Old-Fashioned Chocolate Fudge

450 g/1 lb granulated sugar
150 ml/$\frac{1}{4}$ pint single cream or milk
100 g/4 oz plain, unsweetened chocolate
1 tablespoon golden syrup
50 g/2 oz butter
$\frac{1}{2}$-1 teaspoon vanilla essence
To decorate
walnut halves (optional)

Put all the ingredients, except the walnuts, into a strong saucepan and stir over a low heat until the sugar has dissolved.

Continue as Vanilla Fudge 1 on page 20. When the fudge just begins to set in the tin, mark it into neat pieces with a sharp knife and press a walnut half into each portion if desired. Leave in the tin until quite firm.

Tutti Frutti Fudge

Use any Vanilla Fudge recipe (page 20) based upon 450 g/1 lb
sugar and allow
75 g/3 oz glacé cherries, chopped
75 g/3 oz sultanas
75 g/3 oz mixed nuts, chopped
50 g/2 oz mixed candied peel, chopped

Make the fudge as the recipe. When it reaches a 'really soft ball'
stage or 113 c/236 f, add the remaining ingredients. Mix
thoroughly then heat until the 'soft ball' stage or 114 c/238 f is
reached. Continue as Vanilla Fudge 1 on page 20.

Date and Mandarin Fudge

150 ml/$\frac{1}{4}$ pint water
400 g/14 oz granulated sugar
50 g/2 oz glucose
150 ml/$\frac{1}{4}$ pint full-cream evaporated (unsweetened) canned milk
50 g/2 oz peel from mandarin oranges*
40 g/1$\frac{1}{2}$ oz butter
50 g/2 oz dates, chopped

* or tangerines

Put the water, sugar, glucose and evaporated milk into a strong
saucepan over a gentle heat. Stir until the sugar dissolves then
allow to boil, stirring from time to time, until the mixture reaches a
'really soft ball' stage, or 113 c/236 f (a little softer than is used for
fudge).

Meanwhile, remove all the pith from the mandarin peel before
weighing this; chop the peel very finely, add this and the butter to
the other ingredients, stir well then bring the fudge just to boiling
point. Remove from the heat and beat until creamy. Stir in the
dates then continue as Vanilla Fudge 1, page 20.

The recipes on this and the next few pages are for ultra-luxurious fudge. The recipes contain cream, liqueurs and interesting mixtures of fruit.

Extra Rich Vanilla Fudge

450 g/1 lb granulated sugar
300 ml/$\frac{1}{2}$ pint double cream
50 g/2 oz butter
3 tablespoons water
150 ml/$\frac{1}{4}$ pint milk
1-2 teaspoons vanilla essence or 1 vanilla pod, halved.

Put all the ingredients into a strong saucepan, stir *very carefully* over a low heat until the sugar has dissolved; the high percentage of milk and cream in this recipe makes it burn very readily. Continue as Vanilla Fudge 1, page 20, stirring frequently. Do not exceed the 'really soft ball' stage or 113 c/236 f if you like a very soft fudge, for which this recipe is suitable. For a firmer fudge cook to the 'soft ball' stage or 114 c/238 f.

If using the halved vanilla pod remove at the end of the cooking period, rinse in cold water, allow to dry then store in a jar of sugar. The sugar becomes impregnated with vanilla flavour.

VARIATIONS

Extra Rich Almond Fudge: chop 100-175 g/4-6 oz blanched almonds, add just before the 'really soft ball' stage is reached. Press a blanched almond on top of each marked square when the fudge is partially set.

Extra Rich Apricot Brandy Fudge: use 3 tablespoons apricot brandy instead of the water in the recipe.

Extra Rich Brandy Fudge: use 3 tablespoons brandy instead of the water in the recipe.

Extra Rich Cherry Brandy Fudge: use 3 tablespoons cherry brandy instead of the water in the recipe. Chop 100 g/4 oz glacé cherries, add just before the mixture reaches the 'really soft ball' stage, 113 c/236 f.

Extra Rich Coffee Fudge: blend 1 tablespoon instant coffee powder with the 3 tablespoons water in the recipe.

Extra Rich Fruit Fudge: add about 175 g/6 oz mixed dried fruit just before the mixture reaches the 'really soft ball' stage.

Extra Rich Rum Fudge: use 2 tablespoons rum and 1 tablespoon water instead of the 3 tablespoons water in the recipe.

Fruit Cream Fudge

15 g/$\frac{1}{2}$ oz butter
350 g/12 oz castor sugar
150 ml/$\frac{1}{4}$ pint double cream
$\frac{1}{2}$ teaspoon vanilla essence (optional)
25 g/1 oz glacé pineapple, finely chopped
25 g/1 oz glacé cherries, finely chopped
25 g/1 oz preserved ginger, finely chopped
50 g/2 oz crystallized orange and lemon slices, finely chopped

Put the butter, sugar and cream into a strong saucepan. Stir over a low heat until the sugar has dissolved, then boil steadily, stirring frequently, until the 'soft ball' stage or 114c/238f is reached. Remove from the heat, add the vanilla essence (if using this) and all the other ingredients. Beat well until the mixture turns cloudy.

Grease a 20 × 30-cm/8 × 12-in tin with butter, spoon in the fudge, smooth flat on top with a palette knife. Allow to cool slightly then mark into squares. When set wrap each piece in waxed paper or foil if storing for any length of time.

Creamy Chocolate Fudge

450 g/1 lb granulated sugar
300 ml/½ pint double cream
50 g/2 oz butter
3 tablespoons water
150 ml/¼ pint milk
225 g/8 oz plain chocolate

Put all the ingredients, except the chocolate, into a strong saucepan; stir over a low heat until the sugar dissolves. Break the chocolate into pieces, add to the sugar mixture, stir well to blend with the other ingredients. Allow to boil steadily, stirring quite frequently, until the mixture reaches 'soft ball' stage or 114 c/238 f. It is a more pleasant fudge if it is kept rather soft so never exceed the stage or temperature above.

Continue as Vanilla Fudge 1, page 20.

VARIATIONS

Creamy Chocolate Almond Fudge: chop 100 g/4 oz blanched almonds, add to the other ingredients just before the 'soft ball' stage is reached.

Creamy Chocolate Brazil Fudge: chop 100 g/4 oz Brazil nuts, add just before the 'soft ball' stage is reached.

Creamy Chocolate Hazelnut Fudge: skin 100 g/4 oz hazelnuts, see page 15, then chop and add to the other ingredients just before the 'soft ball' stage is reached.

Creamy Chocolate Vanilla Fudge: add 1 teaspoon vanilla essence to the other ingredients.

Creamy Chocolate Walnut Fudge: chop 100 g/4 oz walnuts, add to the other ingredients just before the 'soft ball' stage is reached.

Creamy Tia Maria Chocolate Fudge: omit 2 tablespoons water from the recipe above and substitute 2 tablespoons Tia Maria liqueur; 100 g/4 oz chopped walnuts and 50 g/2 oz seedless raisins could be added.

Luxury Mocha Fudge

450 g/1 lb granulated sugar
300 ml/½ pint double cream
50 g/2 oz butter
150 ml/¼ pint very strong black coffee
225 g/8 oz plain chocolate

Put all the ingredients, except the chocolate, into a strong saucepan, stir *very carefully* over a low heat until the sugar has dissolved. Break the chocolate into pieces then add to the sugar mixture; continue as Vanilla Fudge 1, page 20.

VARIATIONS

Luxury Mocha Nut Fudge: add approximately 100 g/4 oz chopped blanched almonds, Brazil nuts, hazelnuts or walnuts to the fudge just before setting point is reached.

Brandy Fudge

A Brandy Fudge is given under the Extra Rich Fudge on page 26. It is an excellent flavouring also for the Creamy Chocolate Fudge and variations on page 28 and for the Luxury Mocha Fudge on this page. Substitute brandy for the water in the Creamy Chocolate Fudge; use 3 tablespoons less coffee and substitute brandy in the recipe above.

TO COAT IN FUDGE

Fudge is not really a coating sweetmeat, it is too thick and crumbly. You can, however, ensure an even distribution of nuts and glacé cherries if you do not mix these with the sweetmeat, but place them at even intervals in the lightly buttered or oiled tin, then pour or spoon on the fudge.

UNCOOKED FUDGE

The following recipes produce a soft sweetmeat that is not unlike a true fudge. It is advisable to base most of the recipes upon a chocolate flavour.

Uncooked Chocolate Nut Fudge

225 g/8 oz plain chocolate
25 g/1 oz butter
1 egg
6 tablespoons full-cream condensed (sweetened) canned milk
450 g/1 lb icing sugar, sifted
100 g/4 oz mixed nuts, chopped
$\frac{1}{2}$ teaspoon vanilla essence

Break the chocolate into small pieces, put into a basin with the butter and egg. Stand over a pan of hot, but not boiling, water. Stir briskly, or whisk, until the chocolate has melted and the mixture is thick and creamy.

Add the remaining ingredients. Remove from the heat and beat the mixture until it becomes cloudy and begins to thicken.

Grease a 20-cm/8-in square sandwich tin with a little butter, put in the mixture and leave for several hours until set, then mark into squares.

Uncooked Chocolate Orange Nut Fudge

100 g/4 oz plain chocolate
50 g/2 oz butter
4 tablespoons full-cream evaporated (unsweetened) canned milk
grated rind of 1 orange
100 g/4 oz mixed nuts, chopped
450 g/1 lb icing sugar, sifted

Break the chocolate into pieces, put into a basin with the butter and stand over a pan of hot, but not boiling, water until the chocolate has melted. Remove from the heat, add the milk, orange rind and nuts. Mix well then gradually work in the icing sugar.

Grease a shallow 19 × 29-cm/$7\frac{1}{2}$ × $11\frac{1}{2}$-in tin with a little butter. Put in the mixture, spread flat; allow to set then cut into squares.

Uncooked Vanilla Fudge

100 g/4 oz butter or margarine
100 g/4 oz granulated sugar
4 tablespoons golden syrup
$\frac{1}{4}$-$\frac{1}{2}$ teaspoon vanilla essence
12 tablespoons full-cream dried milk powder

Put all the ingredients except the dried milk powder into a saucepan and stir over a low heat until the sugar has dissolved. Remove from the heat and add the dried milk powder. Mix well with a spoon then with the fingertips.

Grease a 15-18-cm/6-7-in square tin with a little butter; press the mixture into the tin and allow to become quite cold, then mark into squares.

VARIATIONS

Uncooked Chocolate Fudge: add 100 g/4 oz plain chocolate to the dissolved sugar mixture; when the chocolate has melted stir in the dried milk powder. Continue as above.

Uncooked Coffee Fudge: add 2 teaspoons instant coffee powder to the dissolved sugar mixture then stir in the dried milk powder. Continue as above.

TO MAKE PANOCHA

This is very like fudge but the mixture is richer and darker because demerara sugar is used in place of part, or all, white sugar.

Use any of the recipes on pages 20 to 31 following the same method of heating, stirring and beating as for fudge. The following recipe is, however, particularly suitable for the use of demerara sugar.

Panocha

350 g/12 oz demerara sugar
100 g/4 oz granulated sugar
1 (170-g/6-oz) can full-cream evaporated (unsweetened) milk
1 tablespoon golden syrup
1 tablespoon water
25 g/1 oz butter
½ teaspoon vanilla essence
50-100 g/2-4 oz mixed nuts, chopped

Put all the ingredients, except the nuts, into a strong saucepan and stir over a low heat until the sugars have dissolved. Boil steadily, stirring from time to time, until the mixture reaches 'soft ball' stage or 114 c/238 f. Add the nuts then beat until cloudy. Continue as Vanilla Fudge 1 on page 20.

VARIATIONS

Barbados Pineapple Panocha: use 225 g/8 oz Barbados (moist brown) sugar and 225 g/8 oz granulated sugar, 1 (170-g/6-oz) can full-cream evaporated milk, 50 g/2 oz butter and 1 teaspoon vanilla essence. Drain and chop 100 g/4 oz canned pineapple.

Put all these ingredients into a strong saucepan, stir until the sugars have dissolved then boil steadily, stirring from time to time, until the 'soft ball' stage or 114 c/238 f is reached.

Chop 100 g/4 oz walnuts, stir into the mixture, beat until cloudy. Continue as Vanilla Fudge 1 on page 20.

Chocolate Walnut Panocha: follow the basic recipe above but add 50 g/2 oz plain chocolate to the sugar mixture when it has melted. Use chopped walnuts in place of mixed nuts.

Spiced Panocha: follow the basic recipe above but omit the chopped nuts and flavour the mixture with 1 teaspoon vanilla essence, ½-1 teaspoon ground mixed spice and ½-1 teaspoon ground cinnamon.

Ground ginger could be substituted for the mixed spice and cinnamon.

From the top: Raspberry Noyeau, Nougat Montélimar, Chocolate Walnut Panocha and Chiffon Fudge

Candy

The ingredients used and the method of making candy and fudge are somewhat similar. The difference is that fudge is essentially a soft creamy sweetmeat, while candy can be less creamy; it is always crisper and firmer in texture than a good fudge.

METHOD OF MAKING CANDY
While some special candy recipes are more economical than those used for fudge, it is quite possible to take a fudge recipe and make candy from it. The different texture is achieved by boiling the mixture to a slightly higher temperature, that is $115.5c/240f$ instead of $114.4c/238f$, and maintaining the mixture at this temperature for one or two minutes. The different appearance of candy – clear rather than the cloudy look of fudge – is caused by the fact that a candy mixture is not beaten in the saucepan before being poured into the greased tin to set.

USE OF CANDY
Candy is used as a sweetmeat by itself or it can be coated with chocolate. Some candy has a very sweet taste and is better coated with a rather bitter type of chocolate.

DISADVANTAGES OF CANDY
Candy can dry so much with keeping that it becomes crumb-like and can break into pieces very easily.

PROBLEMS OF MAKING CANDY
These are similar to those experienced when making fudge although there is less possibility of the mixture burning in the pan if an economical recipe is used.

TO STORE CANDY
Candy is stored like fudge, see the comments on page 19.

REHEATING CANDY
It is not advisable to reheat this sweetmeat, for it makes it ultra hard and dry.

Clockwise, from the left: Toasted Coconut Caramels, Russian Caramels and Fruit Toffee, Brazil Nut Toffee

Vanilla Candy

1 (397-g/14-oz) can full-cream condensed (sweetened) milk
water (see below)
50 g/2 oz butter or margarine
1 teaspoon vanilla essence
450 g/1 lb granulated sugar

Pour the condensed milk into the saucepan; fill the can with water, add this to the condensed milk together with the butter or margarine, essence and sugar. Stir over a low heat until the sugar has dissolved, then boil steadily, stirring only occasionally, until the mixture reaches the 'soft ball' stage – 116c/240f – but very slightly firmer than for fudge. If you like a softish candy remove the pan from the heat at once; if you prefer a crisper sweetmeat boil slowly (so the temperature will not rise) for 1-2 minutes.

Grease a 20-cm/8-in square tin with a little butter or margarine. Pour in the unbeaten mixture; allow to become almost cold then mark into squares.

Baked Nut Candy

2 egg whites
225 g/8 oz demerara sugar
$\frac{1}{2}$ teaspoon vanilla essence
100 g/4 oz mixed nuts, finely chopped

Whisk the egg whites until very stiff, gradually beat in the sugar then fold in the vanilla essence and nuts. Prepare one or two baking trays as for Meringues (see page 121).

Put teaspoons of the mixture on the trays then bake and store as for Meringues.

VARIATIONS

Chocolate Nut Candy: blend 50 g/2 oz chocolate powder with the sugar.

Coffee Nut Candy: blend 1-2 teaspoons instant coffee powder with the sugar.

VARIATIONS ON VANILLA CANDY

Follow the recipe opposite but make the adaptations below.

The recipes for Vanilla Fudge on page 20 make excellent candy, providing the mixture is allowed to reach 116c/240f, held at this temperature for 1-2 minutes, then poured into the prepared tin without beating.

Butterscotch Candy: use 350 g/12 oz brown (preferably demerara) sugar and 100 g/4 oz golden syrup instead of granulated sugar.

Chocolate Candy: use only $\frac{1}{2}$ teaspoon vanilla essence; add 50 g/2 oz sifted cocoa powder or 100 g/4 oz chocolate powder or 100 g/4 oz chopped plain chocolate to the mixture when the sugar has dissolved and the mixture reaches boiling point.

Coconut Candy: add 175 g/6 oz desiccated or finely grated fresh coconut to the mixture when the sugar has dissolved.

Fig Candy: chop 100 g/4 oz dried figs very finely; add to the mixture when the sugar has dissolved.

Ginger Candy: chop 100 g/4 oz crystallized or well-drained preserved ginger. Add to the mixture, together with 1-2 teaspoons ground ginger when the sugar has dissolved.

Nut Candy: chop 100-175 g/4-6 oz nuts; add to the mixture just before the 'soft ball' stage is reached.

Raspberry Candy: omit the vanilla essence and add 1-1$\frac{1}{2}$ teaspoons raspberry essence when the 'soft ball' stage is reached. Strawberry or other essences could be used in place of raspberry.

Nougat or Noyeau

Nougat is a sweet that is not particularly difficult to make but it needs careful attention to the various stages of heating. Its sweet, slightly sticky texture makes it a delicious sweetmeat.

METHODS OF MAKING NOUGAT

The traditional method of making nougat is to boil together sugar and water with golden syrup until it reaches the 'firm to very firm ball' stage (121-132c/250-270f) then add whisked egg whites, warmed honey and nuts. The inclusion of golden syrup and honey makes the deliciously 'chewy' type of nougat. It is traditional to put the sweetmeat mixture between sheets of rice paper but this is not essential, see page 40.

There are several variations on this recipe, including one that needs far less cooking, see page 42.

USE OF NOUGAT

Nougat is generally a sweet by itself although it can be coated with chocolate; it is too sweet in flavour to be coated with fondant.

DISADVANTAGES OF NOUGAT

There are really no disadvantages to making nougat, except that you must become skilled at incorporating the egg whites. The sweetmeat does tend to become harder if exposed to the air, so should be stored carefully.

PROBLEMS OF MAKING NOUGAT

Make sure the sugar mixture has reached the temperature given in the recipe before it is incorporated with the whisked egg whites. Beat all the time while adding the sugar mixture to the egg whites.

TO STORE NOUGAT

If you are not using rice paper, wrap individual pieces of nougat in waxed or greaseproof paper. Store in airtight tins or boxes.

TO REHEAT NOUGAT

This is inadvisable when egg whites are used, since reheating destroys the light texture of the sweetmeat.

Almond Nougat

A firm nougat that is rather exceptional for it does not contain honey.

450 g/1 lb granulated sugar
25 g/1 oz butter
150 ml/¼ pint water
2 egg whites
175 g/6 oz almonds, blanched and cut into narrow strips
To coat and cover
rice paper or wafers

Put the sugar, butter and water into a strong saucepan. Stir over a moderate heat until the sugar has dissolved. Boil steadily until the mixture reaches 'firm ball' stage or 121 c/250 f.

While the sugar mixture is boiling, put the egg whites into a large ovenproof mixing bowl and whisk until very stiff. Stand the bowl over a saucepan of boiling water; gradually pour the sugar mixture on to the egg whites, stirring well as you do so. Add the almonds, stir over the heat then test again to check the mixture has once more reached 'firm ball' stage or 121 c/250 f. Continue as Golden Nougat on page 40.

VARIATIONS

Make the recipe as above but heat 2 tablespoons honey; blend with the sugar and whisked egg white mixture, as described in Golden Nougat.

Cherry Almond Nougat: recipe as above but reduce the almonds to 75-100 g/3-4 oz and add 75 g/3 oz chopped glacé cherries.

Raspberry Nougat: add up to ¼ teaspoon raspberry essence to the mixture. Other essences can be used instead.

Raspberry Bulgarian Nougat: omit the butter and water in the Almond Nougat recipe, but add 225 g/8 oz liquid glucose to the sugar. Stir over a low heat until the sugar has dissolved then allow to boil and continue as the Almond Nougat recipe. In addition to the almonds add 75 g/3 oz chopped glacé cherries and 50 g/2 oz chopped angelica together with a few drops of raspberry essence.

Golden Nougat

This is a very sweet chewy nougat.

450 g/1 lb granulated sugar
150 ml/¼ pint water
3 tablespoons golden syrup
pinch cream of tartar
3 tablespoons honey
4 egg whites
100 g/4 oz pistachio nuts, blanched and chopped
few drops vanilla essence
To coat and cover
rice paper or wafers

Put the sugar, water and golden syrup into a strong saucepan, stir over a moderate heat until the sugar has dissolved. Boil steadily until the mixture reaches 'very firm ball' stage or 132 c/270 f. Stir in the cream of tartar.

While the sugar and golden syrup mixture is boiling, put the honey into a saucepan over very low heat, or use the top of a double saucepan or a basin over boiling water. Heat until the honey is very hot. Put the egg whites into a large ovenproof mixing bowl and whisk until very stiff. Lift the mixing bowl over a saucepan of boiling water; gradually pour the golden syrup mixture on to the egg whites, stirring very well as you do so. When thoroughly blended, add the hot honey, chopped nuts and vanilla essence. Stir the mixture for a few minutes then test again. At this stage the nougat should be at 'firm ball' stage or 121 c/250 f (lower than the temperature initially).

If too soft continue to heat over the hot water and test again; never transfer the mixture to a saucepan. Line a 23-25-cm/9-10-in square tin with rice paper or ice cream wafers. Pour the mixture into the tin, cover with more rice paper or wafers. Allow to set, cut into neat pieces and wrap in waxed paper.

VARIATION

Use the recipe above but omit the golden syrup. This gives a whiter and firmer nougat.

Nougat Montélimar

450 g/1 lb loaf or granulated sugar
40 g/1½ oz liquid glucose
150 ml/¼ pint water
350 g/12 oz honey, preferably clear
1½ large or 2 small egg whites
150 g/5 oz icing sugar, sifted
175 g/6 oz almonds, blanched and coarsely chopped
50-100 g/2-4 oz pistachio nuts, blanched and halved
100 g/4 oz glacé cherries, chopped
To coat and cover
rice paper

Put the sugar, glucose and water into a strong saucepan, stir over a low heat until the sugar has dissolved. Boil, without stirring, until the mixture reaches 'crack' stage or 138 c/280 f. While the sugar mixture is boiling put the honey into a second saucepan and boil until it reaches 'firm ball' stage or 121 c/250 f. Put the egg whites into an ovenproof mixing bowl, whisk until they are very stiff, then gradually pour the very hot sugar mixture on to the egg whites, beating all the time. When the sugar mixture has been incorporated beat in the hot honey and then the icing sugar. Finally add the nuts and cherries.

Line a 20-23-cm/8-9-in square tin with rice paper; pour in the hot nougat. Top with more rice paper, cool slightly, then cover the surface with a weight. Leave for 24 hours; cut into oblong shapes. Wrap in waxed paper and store in an airtight tin.

VARIATIONS

Add 1-2 teaspoons orange flower water (obtainable from a chemist) and omit this amount of water.

Omit the glucose (this helps to give a shiny and slightly sticky nougat) and add a pinch of cream of tartar instead.

Reduce the honey to 150 g/5 oz to give a less sticky nougat.

Creamy Nougat: use 150 ml/¼ pint single cream in place of the water in the recipe; this is particularly delicious. Use 3 tablespoons Italian Meringue mixture (before baking, see page 121) instead of the egg whites.

EASY NOUGAT

The recipe that follows is for a type of nougat that needs the minimum of cooking, but it has the lightness of true nougat.

The name 'noyeau' doubtless comes from 'noyau', which is the name of a brandy in which fruit kernels are infused. You could replace the raspberry essence with a little apricot noyau if you wish. The second recipe for a Raspberry Noyeau is on page 108 in the section dealing with truffles. It could be described as a truffle-type nougat.

Raspberry Noyeau I

225 g/8 oz icing sugar, sifted
$\frac{1}{2}$ teaspoon raspberry essence
75 g/3 oz honey
$\frac{1}{2}$ tablespoon glucose
3 egg whites
175 g/6 oz almonds, blanched and chopped
50 g/2 oz glacé cherries, chopped
pink colouring (optional)
To coat and cover
25 g/1 oz icing sugar, sifted
rice paper

Put the sugar, essence, honey and glucose into a large ovenproof mixing bowl and stand over a saucepan of boiling water. Heat until the mixture is like a syrup. Whisk the egg whites in another bowl until very stiff, then add to the sugar mixture. Continue to beat over the heat until the sweetmeat becomes very thick. Add the almonds and cherries and any colouring required. Allow to cool slightly.

Dust an 18-cm/7-in square tin with half the icing sugar, then cover with rice paper. Spoon in the nougat mixture, top with more rice paper and icing sugar. Put a light weight over the top and leave until cold, then cut into neat bars.

CHAPTER 2

HARD AND CHEWY

The wide range of sweetmeats covered in this chapter begins with caramels. There is not only considerable variety in the way caramels can be flavoured, but, by adjusting the heat to which the mixture is boiled, you produce soft, medium, hard or very hard caramels. The information about making these popular sweets is given below and on page 44.

The next section, which begins on page 50, is for toffees of all kinds, including the children's favourite – Toffee Apples. Children enjoy making toffee, but the mixture has to be cooked to a very high temperature, so an adult should be in charge of the operation. After toffee comes hard nut brittle and butterscotch, followed by a section on boiled sweets, which includes traditional humbugs, acid drops, fruit drops and barley sugar. Children enjoy sweet lollies and you will find the method of making these on page 69.

The section ends with pralines. Although the ingredients used, and temperature to which the mixture is boiled, are very similar to that required for candy, the initial stage of caramelling the sugar or syrup in the recipe gives this sweetmeat its distinctive taste and texture.

Caramels

These sweets are very much enjoyed by most children, as they last a long time in the mouth and have a good firm texture. They can be varied by adding other ingredients, see page 45.

METHOD OF MAKING CARAMELS

Caramels are made by boiling liquid (water and milk or cream) with sugar; glucose and/or cream of tartar are added and some recipes contain butter.

USE OF CARAMELS

Caramels are a sweetmeat in themselves or can be coated with chocolate; they are rarely used as part of other sweetmeats.

DISADVANTAGES OF CARAMELS

Caramels are quite difficult to cut. One can buy special caramel cutters, but, providing the sweetmeat is marked firmly when it is half set, it is not difficult to cut the cold sweetmeat neatly with a sharp knife.

PROBLEMS OF MAKING CARAMELS

Careful attention to temperature is essential. If you intend to make caramels frequently you are well advised to buy a sugar thermometer, since the temperature to which the mixture has to boil is a little difficult for the beginner to ascertain.

It must be remembered that there are various stages to which one can boil the mixture; the texture that pleases one person will not necessarily please another. The mixture for a soft caramel should reach 'firm ball' stage or 121.1 c/250 f; for a moderately firm caramel allow the mixture to reach 'firmer ball' stage or 126.6 c/260 f; for a really firm hard caramel allow the mixture to reach 'very firm ball' stage or 129.4-132.2 c/265-270 f (also known as 'light crack' or 'soft crack').

Caramel is a sweetmeat that must be stirred well to dissolve the sugar, then stirred from time to time as the mixture cooks. Make sure the saucepan is sufficiently large to facilitate cooking evenly and rapidly.

The correct use of glucose or cream of tartar in the recipes prevents a tendency for the mixture to become gritty, but too much glucose will hinder the mixture from setting. A temperature of one degree Celsius or two degrees Fahrenheit higher than given in the recipe should be used when making caramels in very hot weather, so that they will harden as the mixture cools.

TO STORE CARAMELS

It is advisable to wrap each caramel in waxed paper to retain the correct texture. Caramels coated in chocolate do not need wrapping. Store in an airtight tin or box.

TO REHEAT CARAMELS

This mixture is not suitable for habitual storage and reheating. If, however, a batch of caramels has become over-sticky due to exposure to the air, put them into a saucepan and stir continually until the mixture melts, then bring up to the temperature given in the original recipe.

Creamy Vanilla Caramels

450 g/1 lb granulated sugar
150 ml/¼ pint milk
150 ml/¼ pint full-cream evaporated (unsweetened) canned milk
or single cream
1 teaspoon vanilla essence
75 g/3 oz glucose
pinch cream of tartar

Put all the ingredients, except the glucose and cream of tartar, into a strong saucepan. Stir over a low heat until the sugar has dissolved, then boil the mixture steadily for 2-3 minutes. Blend in the glucose and cream of tartar and continue to boil steadily, stirring from time to time, until the mixture reaches 'firm ball' stage, or 121 c/250 f for a soft caramel. If you prefer a harder caramel, see the information opposite. Do not beat the mixture, it should not be cloudy like fudge.

Grease a 20-cm/8-in square sandwich tin with a little butter, pour in the mixture. Allow to cool and become partially set then mark the sweetmeat into sections. Leave in the tin until quite cold, then wrap each sweetmeat in waxed paper.

VARIATIONS

Butter Caramels: use the ingredients above but melt 75 g/3 oz butter with the sugar mixture.

Creamy Chocolate Caramels: increase the amount of ordinary milk to 300 ml/½ pint. Chop 175 g/6 oz plain chocolate into small pieces, add to the mixture with the glucose and cream of tartar. Since chocolate helps to set a sweetmeat, allow the mixture to reach only 'slightly firm ball' stage or 120 c/248 f, for a really soft caramel.

Creamy Coffee Caramels: use 150 ml/¼ pint strong black coffee instead of the milk in the basic recipe above.

Opera Caramels: use raspberry essence instead of vanilla and colour the mixture pale pink.

Rich Vanilla Caramels

450 g/1 lb granulated or loaf sugar
1 (397-g/14-oz) can full-cream condensed (sweetened) milk
2 tablespoons water
100 g/4 oz butter
25 g/1 oz golden syrup
1 teaspoon vanilla essence
pinch cream of tartar

Put all the ingredients, except the cream of tartar, into a strong saucepan. Stir over a low heat until the sugar has dissolved, then boil for 2-3 minutes. Blend in the cream of tartar and continue to boil steadily, stirring from time to time, until the mixture reaches 'firm ball' stage or 121 C/250 F, for a soft caramel. If you prefer a harder caramel, see the information on page 44.

Continue as Creamy Vanilla Caramels on page 45.

VARIATIONS ON CARAMELS

These recipes are based on any of the caramel recipes, using 450 g/1 lb sugar.

Coconut Caramels: blend 100-175 g/4-6 oz desiccated coconut with the mixture just before it reaches 'firm ball' stage.

Ginger Caramels: blend 1-2 teaspoons ground ginger with the sugar. Finely chop 100 g/4 oz crystallized or well-drained preserved ginger. Add to the mixture just before it reaches 'firm ball' stage.

Nut Caramels: to 450 g/1 lb sugar allow 100-175 g/4-6 oz nuts. These can be mixed or of one kind. Chop the nuts and add to the mixture just before it reaches 'firm ball' stage.

Russian Caramels

450 g/1 lb demerara sugar
1 (397-g/14-oz) can full-cream condensed (sweetened) milk
100 g/4 oz butter
1 teaspoon vanilla essence

Put all the ingredients into a strong saucepan, stir over a low heat until the sugar has dissolved. Boil steadily, stirring from time to time until the mixture reaches 'firm ball' stage, 121 c/250 f. This should be a soft type of caramel, but if you prefer a firmer sweetmeat, see page 44.

Continue as Creamy Vanilla Caramels on page 45.

Russian Toffee

A toffee-caramel.

275 g/10 oz granulated sugar
175 g/6 oz moist light brown sugar
1 tablespoon glucose
2 tablespoons honey
6 tablespoons single cream
4 tablespoons water
175 g/6 oz butter
$\frac{1}{2}$-1 teaspoon vanilla essence

Place the sugars, glucose, honey, cream, water and 50 g/2 oz of the butter in a strong saucepan. Stir over a low heat until the sugars have dissolved, then boil steadily, stirring frequently until the mixture reaches 'soft ball' stage, 116 c/240 f. Gradually add the rest of the butter with the vanilla essence. Boil to 'firm ball' stage, 124 c/256 f. This is the setting for a soft to moderately firm caramel; although termed a toffee, this really is a caramel.

Grease a 20-cm/8-in square sandwich tin, pour in the mixture. Leave until lightly set then mark into squares. Cut the squares firmly again when the sweetmeat is cold and wrap in waxed paper.

This is a good toffee for coating in chocolate.

Syrup Chocolate Caramels

75 g/3 oz butter or margarine
150 ml/¼ pint full-cream condensed (sweetened) canned milk
225 g/8 oz granulated sugar
8 tablespoons golden syrup
½ teaspoon vanilla essence
100 g/4 oz plain chocolate

Put all the ingredients, except the chocolate, into a strong saucepan. Stir over a low heat until the sugar has dissolved. Chop the chocolate into pieces, add to the sugar mixture, then boil steadily, stirring from time to time until the mixture reaches 'slightly firm ball' stage or 120 c/248 f for a really soft caramel (the chocolate helps the sweetmeat to set). If you prefer a harder caramel see the information on page 44. Do not beat the mixture, it should not be cloudy like fudge.

Continue as Creamy Vanilla Caramels on page 45.

VARIATION

Treacle Chocolate Caramels: use black treacle instead of golden syrup.

Redcurrant Russian Caramels

ingredients as Russian Caramels (page 47) but use granulated sugar instead of demerara sugar
3 tablespoons redcurrant jelly

Prepare and cook the mixture as given under Russian Caramels. Allow the mixture to reach 'firm ball' stage or 121 c/250 f then add the redcurrant jelly and blend with the mixture. Continue as Creamy Vanilla Caramels on page 45.

Scotch Toffee

A toffee-caramel.

450 g/1 lb granulated sugar
150 ml/¼ pint plus 4 tablespoons water
50 g/2 oz butter
1 (198-g/7-oz) can full-cream condensed (sweetened) milk
1 teaspoon vanilla essence

Put all the ingredients into a strong saucepan, stir over a low heat until the sugar has dissolved. Boil until the mixture reaches 'firm ball' stage or 121 c/250 f. This is the setting for a soft caramel.

Grease an oblong tin, approximately 19 × 29 × 1 cm/7½ × 11¼ × ½ in, with a little melted butter. Pour in the mixture, leave until lightly set, then mark into squares. Break or cut again when cold. A shallow 1-cm/½-in sweetmeat is usual in this recipe. Wrap in waxed paper.

Toasted Coconut Caramels

450 g/1 lb castor sugar
150 ml/¼ pint water
pinch cream of tartar
100 g/4 oz desiccated coconut

Put the sugar, water and cream of tartar into a strong saucepan. Stir over a steady heat until the mixture reaches a 'fairly firm ball' stage or 118 c/245 f. Add the coconut and stir until the mixture becomes cloudy. Grease an 18-cm/7-in square sandwich tin with butter, pour in the mixture; when nearly cold cut into 2.5-cm/1-in squares. Leave in the tin until cold, remove and place on a large baking tray.

Toast under a preheated grill for a few seconds, turn and toast on the second, then on the third and fourth sides. Allow to cool then store in an airtight tin.

Toffee

These are possibly one of the greatest favourites with most people, particularly children; toffee is comparatively simple to make. Some toffees do become sticky with storage so large amounts should not be made.

METHOD OF MAKING TOFFEE

Toffee recipes vary appreciably. In most recipes butter, sugar and water are boiled to a high temperature. In other recipes golden syrup or treacle are added. The mixture should be stirred as little as possible. The temperature to which toffee should be brought is a very high one, in most cases it is the 'hard crack' stage, i.e., 143.3c/290f. In the recipes the decimal point is omitted but make sure you reach the correct temperature on a Celsius thermometer.

USE OF TOFFEE

Generally as a sweetmeat by itself or coated with chocolate.

DISADVANTAGES OF TOFFEE

Great care should be taken when testing for the right temperature, but apart from this there are few problems with toffees.

Because of the very high boiling point to which the sugar mixture should be brought, many toffees can become sticky even if stored in tins.

PROBLEMS OF MAKING TOFFEE

Because the mixture is boiled to a very high temperature, care should be taken that it does not over-heat and burn or splash over the sides of the pan.

TO STORE TOFFEE

The toffee in one or two cases is unsuitable for keeping but this information is stated clearly in the recipes; in other recipes the toffees should be individually wrapped in waxed paper before storage. Store carefully in airtight tins or containers.

TO REHEAT TOFFEE

Most toffee mixtures are not suitable for reheating.

Opposite *Clockwise, from the left*: Butterscotch, Barley Sugar Sticks and Edinburgh Rock, Peanut Brittle
Overleaf *From the top*: Acid Drops, Sugar Lollies, Toffee Apples, Harlequin Humbugs

Almond Syrup Toffee

A slightly sticky toffee.

350 g/12 oz granulated sugar
75 g/3 oz butter
150 g/5 oz golden syrup
150 ml/¼ pint water
75 g/3 oz almonds, blanched and finely chopped

Put all the ingredients, except the almonds, into a strong saucepan and stir over a moderate heat until the sugar has dissolved. Boil fairly briskly until the mixture reaches 'light crack' stage or 138 c/280 f. Remove from the heat and stir the almonds in well.

Grease a 20-cm/8-in square sandwich tin with a little butter, pour in the mixture and allow to set lightly then mark into squares. Do not remove from the tin until cold. This sweetmeat is less brittle than a true toffee, it has a slightly chewy texture. Wrap in waxed paper.

VARIATION

Almond Treacle Toffee: substitute black treacle for golden syrup.

Everton Toffee 1

A buttery toffee.

450 g/1 lb granulated or demerara sugar
100 g/4 oz butter
1 teaspoon lemon juice or white malt vinegar
150 ml/¼ pint water

Put the ingredients into a strong saucepan; stir over a moderate heat until the sugar has dissolved, then continue as Golden Toffee on page 54.

VARIATION

Creamy Everton Toffee: use single cream or milk instead of water in the recipe above.

Everton Toffee 2

100 g/4 oz butter
225 g/8 oz golden syrup
225 g/8 oz demerara sugar

Put the butter into a strong saucepan and stir over a very low heat until melted. Add the syrup and sugar, stir well until dissolved then continue as Golden Toffee, below.

Note Either Everton Toffee 1 or 2 and Golden Toffee can be used as the basis for a number of different flavours, see below and opposite.

Golden Toffee

A good basic recipe.

450 g/1 lb demerara sugar
200 ml/7 fl oz water
40 g/1½ oz butter
2 tablespoons golden syrup
1 teaspoon brown or white malt vinegar

Put all the ingredients into a strong saucepan, stir over a moderate heat until the sugar has dissolved. Boil fairly briskly to the 'hard crack' stage or 143 c/290 f; stir as little as possible.

Grease a 20-cm/8-in square sandwich tin with a little butter, pour in the mixture. Allow to set lightly then mark into squares. Do not remove from the tin until cold. If preferred leave the toffee to set firmly as a slab then break into pieces. Wrap the individual pieces or slab in waxed paper.

VARIATION

Rich Golden Toffee: use 75 g/3 oz butter in the recipe above.

VARIATIONS ON GOLDEN OR EVERTON TOFFEE

Follow the recipe for Golden Toffee or one of the Everton Toffee recipes (pages 53 and 54) with the following adaptations.

Almond Toffee: blanch up to 175 g/6 oz almonds. Chop coarsely and add to the mixture just before it reaches the 'hard crack' stage. The almonds can be left whole and pressed on top of the toffee when it begins to set in the tin.

Brazil Nut Toffee: follow the directions for Almond Toffee above; as Brazils are so large you will need to halve the nuts before pressing on top of the toffee.

Cherry Toffee: halve 100-175 g/4-6 oz glacé cherries, or leave them whole and add to the toffee just before it reaches 'hard crack' stage.

Coconut Toffee: add 100-175 g/4-6 oz desiccated coconut to the toffee mixture after it has come to the boil.

Date Toffee: chop 175 g/6 oz stoned dates; add to the toffee just before it reaches 'hard crack' stage.

Fruit Toffee: you can use all raisins or all sultanas or a mixture of dried fruits. If using large raisins, deseed them and cut into halves or quarters with kitchen scissors. Allow 100-175 g/4-6 oz fruit and add to the toffee just before it reaches 'hard crack' stage. If the fruit is inclined to be dry, put it in the mixture a little earlier; this gives it an opportunity to become more moist.

Ginger Toffee: add 1-2 teaspoons ground ginger to the mixture when the sugar has dissolved.

Peanut Butter Toffee: follow the recipe for Everton Toffee 1, but use 50 g/2 oz butter and 75 g/3 oz peanut butter. Add 175-225 g/ 6-8 oz chopped peanuts just before the mixture reaches 'hard crack' stage.

Peppermint Toffee: add up to 1 teaspoon peppermint essence or a few drops of oil of peppermint to the mixture when the sugar has dissolved. It is wise to be sparing with the quantity of flavouring at first, then add more later if required.

Rum Toffee: if using the Golden Toffee or Everton 1 recipe, omit 1-2 tablespoons water and substitute rum instead. In the Everton Toffee 2 recipe, add the rum to the other ingredients. Up to 1 teaspoon rum essence could be used instead of rum; do not reduce the water in the recipes.

Rum flavouring combines well with fruit and/or nuts.

Honeycomb Toffee

250 g/9 oz granulated sugar
40 g/1½ oz butter or margarine
3 tablespoons golden syrup
3 tablespoons water
6 drops white malt vinegar
1½ teaspoons bicarbonate of soda (the teaspoons *must* be level)

Put the sugar, butter or margarine, syrup and water into a large strong saucepan. It is important to have a large pan because the mixture rises drastically in the pan when the bicarbonate of soda is added.

Stir over a moderate heat until the sugar has dissolved. Boil briskly until the mixture reaches 'hard crack stage' or 143 c/290 f. Stir in the vinegar and bicarbonate of soda.

Grease a 15-18-cm/6-7-in square sandwich tin with a little butter, pour in the mixture. Leave until set and cold then break into pieces. As the name suggests, this toffee has a honeycomb texture.

Note Measure the bicarbonate of soda carefully. It is advisable to make only a small quantity of this toffee at a time since it goes very sticky when kept.

Chocolate Toffee

350 g/12 oz granulated sugar
100 g/4 oz golden syrup
150 ml/¼ pint water
50 g/2 oz butter
175 g/6 oz plain chocolate

Put all the ingredients, except the chocolate, into a strong saucepan; stir over a moderate heat until dissolved. Boil steadily until the mixture reaches 'moderately hard crack' stage or 141 c/286 f. Chocolate helps to set a sweetmeat so you can have a slightly lower stage or temperature.

Chop the chocolate into small pieces, add to the sweetmeat, stir away from the heat until the chocolate has blended with the toffee mixture.

Grease a 20-23-cm/8-9-in square sandwich tin with a little butter, pour in the mixture. Allow to set lightly then mark into squares. Leave in the tin until cold then wrap in waxed paper.

VARIATIONS

Chocolate Orange Toffee: use orange juice instead of water in the recipe above; add 2 teaspoons finely grated orange rind. 175 g/6 oz plain chocolate can be added to Everton Toffee 1 (page 53) or Golden Toffee (page 54) just before the 'hard crack' stage. Everton Toffee 2 has a rather high percentage of golden syrup which is inclined to over-ride the taste of chocolate.

Treacle or Molasses Toffee

Black treacle (molasses) has a very distinct flavour. It is therefore important that this does not become too overwhelming. In the Golden Toffee recipe on page 54 black treacle or molasses can be substituted for the golden syrup.

In any toffee recipe you could use all molasses sugar in place of granulated or demerara sugar to give a strong flavour. The recipe over the page makes a particularly good toffee.

Creamy Treacle Toffee

350 g/12 oz moist light brown sugar
50 g/2 oz butter
75 g/3 oz golden syrup
75 g/3 oz black treacle
6 tablespoons full-cream condensed (sweetened) canned milk
1½ teaspoons brown malt vinegar

Put all the ingredients into a strong saucepan, stir over a low heat until the sugar has dissolved. Boil steadily, stirring occasionally until the mixture reaches 'light crack' stage or 138 c/280 f. This is less hard than most toffees.

Oil a 20-23-cm/8-9-in square sandwich tin and pour in the mixture. Allow to set lightly then mark into squares. Leave in the tin until cold then wrap in waxed paper.

VARIATION

Creamy Toffee: the recipe above makes an excellent creamy toffee if the black treacle is omitted and 175 g/6 oz golden syrup is used instead. 100 g/4 oz chopped nuts can be added.

Peanut Butter Toffee

450 g/1 lb demerara sugar
200 ml/7 fl oz water
40 g/1½ oz butter
75 g/3 oz peanut butter
2 tablespoons golden syrup
1 teaspoon vinegar

Put the sugar, water and butter into a strong saucepan, stir over a low heat until the sugar has dissolved then add the remaining ingredients and thoroughly blend together. Boil to 'hard crack' stage or 143 c/290 f, then continue as Golden Toffee on page 54.

TAFFY

'Taffy' is generally considered to be the old-fashioned name for toffee but the original taffy was frequently a pulled sweet as the recipe below.

Pulled Taffy

225 g/8 oz demerara sugar
175 g/6 oz golden syrup
100 g/4 oz butter
2 tablespoons warm water
2 teaspoons glucose

Put all the ingredients into a strong saucepan; stir over a low heat until the sugar has dissolved. Boil steadily until the mixture reaches 'light crack' stage, 129-131 c/265-268 f. Brush a slab or tin with a little melted butter or oil, pour the hot mixture on to the slab. When cool enough to handle, pull gently until you have made long strips of even thickness. Use just the fingertips to pull the sweetmeat; if it sticks either dampen your fingers or dip them in cornflour.

Cut the taffy into neat pieces with kitchen scissors brushed with melted butter or oil, and wrap in waxed paper.

VARIATIONS

Molasses Taffy: use the amount of sugar and water as in the recipe above. Substitute black treacle for the golden syrup. Omit the butter and glucose and add 1 teaspoon vinegar. Boil the mixture to the 'light crack' stage as above. Remove the pan from the heat, blend in 25 g/1 oz butter and $\frac{1}{4}$ teaspoon bicarbonate of soda. Mix thoroughly then proceed as above.

Peppermint Taffy: use the basic recipe and flavour this with a few drops of oil of peppermint or $\frac{1}{2}$-1 teaspoon peppermint essence.

Other essences e.g. rum or almond could be substituted.

To Make Toffee Apples

1. Choose ripe and perfect dessert apples that are not too large; the ideal apple is sweet and crisp in texture; inspect the fruit carefully to see there are no bruises.

2. As apple skins have a certain amount of natural oil and grease, the fruit should be washed and dried very carefully before coating with toffee.

3. Before starting to make the toffee apples, assemble all the ingredients. The working order should be as follows:

a)   Prepare the apples; insert the wooden sticks.

b)   Have a large container for boiling water available in which to stand the saucepan of cooked toffee so it does not harden in the pan. Check that the container used is suitable to withstand the great heat of the toffee and saucepan.

c)   Have a basin of cold water for testing the toffee.

d)   Prepare a bowl of cold water in which to dip the coated apples so the toffee sets quickly.

e)   Prepare a flat baking sheet or buttered tray on which to stand the apples.

4. Dip the apples into the hot toffee and, if you want a thick coating, hold them over the pan for a moment, then dip them again.

5. Unless the toffee apples are to be eaten immediately after the toffee coating is cold and set, or at least within an hour, it is essential to wrap them in waxed or greaseproof paper. Secure the paper around the apples with a firm twist or an elastic band.

CHOOSING THE TOFFEE

The kind of toffee to use depends on whether you like a brittle or creamier and softer toffee. The Golden Toffee and Everton Toffees 1 and 2 can be used; these recipes will coat 8-10 medium apples. In addition to these toffees, the following recipes give excellent results.

Brittle Toffee for Apples

225 g/8 oz granulated sugar
225 g/8 oz golden syrup
8 dessert apples, unpeeled

Put the ingredients, except the apples, into a strong saucepan and stir over a moderate heat until the sugar has dissolved. Boil until the mixture almost reaches the 'very hard crack' stage, 154 c/310 f. Continue as the directions opposite and coat the apples.

VARIATIONS

Medium Brittle Toffee: use 350 g/12 oz granulated sugar and 75 g/3 oz butter or margarine instead of the ingredients above. Follow the method of cooking as above but boil only to 'hard crack' stage or 143 c/290 f. Coat the eight apples as the instructions opposite.

Creamy Toffee: use 450 g/1 lb demerara or granulated sugar, 50 g/2 oz butter, 150 ml/¼ pint single cream or milk, a pinch of cream of tartar and ½ tablespoon brown malt vinegar. Put all the ingredients into a strong saucepan, stir over a moderate heat until the sugar has dissolved. Boil steadily, stirring from time to time, until the mixture reaches 'hard crack' stage or 143 c/290 f. This recipe produces slightly more toffee than the two recipes above and will coat up to 10 apples.

BRITTLE NUT TOFFEES

There are two ways of preparing an assortment of brittle nut toffees:

a) Make up a succession of smaller quantities, as given in the following recipe, adding one kind of nut to each batch so you have a good selection of toffees, or
b) Make up four or five times the quantity of toffee given in the recipe. Put four or five varieties of nut in four or five containers and quickly pour the hot toffee mixture over the nuts.

Brittle Nut Toffee

450 g/1 lb granulated sugar
150 ml/¼ pint milk
225 g/8 oz butter
225 g/8 oz nuts*, blanched and chopped

*a selection of nuts, see Nut Brittle, below.

Put the ingredients, except the nuts, into a strong saucepan, stir over a moderate heat until the sugar dissolves. Boil fairly briskly until the mixture reaches 'hard crack' stage or 143 c/290 f. Add the nuts just before the mixture reaches this stage.

Lightly grease a flat tin with a little butter or oil. Drop spoonfuls of the nut toffee on to the tin and allow to set. If preferred use several kinds of nuts; put these into individual greased tins and quickly pour over the hot toffee. Leave until firm then break into pieces. Wrap in waxed paper to store or keep in an airtight tin.

Nut Brittle

ingredients as Golden Toffee (page 54)
225 g/8 oz nuts*, blanched and finely chopped

*choose almonds, Brazil nuts, cashew nuts, hazelnuts,
peanuts, pecan nuts, walnuts or mixed nuts.

Make the toffee as the recipe on page 54; add the nuts just before the mixture reaches 'hard crack' stage or 143 c/290 f, mix well with the toffee.

Lightly grease a flat tin with a little butter or oil. Drop spoonfuls of the nut toffee on to the tin and allow to set. If preferred use several kinds of nuts; put these into individual greased tins and quickly pour over the hot toffee. Leave until firm then break into pieces.

Peanut Brittle

The recipe for Brittle Nut Toffee opposite can be used with either fresh or salted peanuts. The latter may sound unusual but the contrast of the salted nuts and sweet toffee is extremely pleasant and interesting. The following recipe, however, is particularly suitable for peanuts. Use fresh or salted nuts. If using fresh nuts blanch them first (see page 15); omit salt with salted nuts.

450 g/1 lb granulated sugar
225 g/8 oz golden syrup
150 ml/$\frac{1}{4}$ pint water
275 g/10 oz peanuts
$\frac{1}{4}$ teaspoon salt
15 g/$\frac{1}{2}$ oz butter
$\frac{1}{4}$ teaspoon bicarbonate of soda

Put the sugar, syrup and water into a large heavy saucepan, stir over a low heat until the sugar has dissolved. Boil until the mixture reaches the 'soft ball' stage or 114 c/238 f. Add the peanuts and salt, then continue to boil until the mixture reaches 'light crack' stage or 138 c/280 f; stir frequently during this stage. Add the butter and bicarbonate of soda, stir to blend; the mixture will bubble quite briskly.

Grease one or two large flat tins with melted butter or oil. Pour the mixture on to the tins then cool this partially by lifting around the edges with a metal spatula. Keep the spatula moving under the mixture so it does not stick to the tins. When it becomes firm but is still warm, turn the brittle completely over. Pull the edges to make the brittle thinner in the centre, allow to become quite cold, then break into pieces. Wrap in waxed paper.

VARIATION

Almond Brittle: omit the peanuts and salt in the recipe. Blanch 225 275 g/8-10 oz almonds and cut into narrow strips; add to the toffee mixture when it reaches 'light crack' stage. A few drops of almond or ratafia essence could be added.

Butterscotch

This section includes nuts, coated or combined with butterscotch, for the same basic recipe applies to all these sweetmeats. Butterscotch is delicious and not particularly difficult to make.

METHOD OF MAKING BUTTERSCOTCH

A good butterscotch, as the name suggests, should contain a high percentage of butter. This is heated with the sugar and water until it reaches the 'brittle' stage, i.e. 138 c/280 f. Recipes do vary; some contain milk, others glucose, others cream of tartar.

USE OF BUTTERSCOTCH

This is a sweetmeat by itself or combined with nuts. Since the sweetmeats are generally large when nuts have been coated, they are rarely coated with chocolate.

DISADVANTAGES OF BUTTERSCOTCH

There are really few disadvantages to plain butterscotch; it is a sweetmeat that is often given to people who feel slightly unwell during travelling. When combined with nuts it does become a fairly costly sweetmeat.

PROBLEMS OF MAKING BUTTERSCOTCH

The very high temperature to which one boils the mixture makes it essential to use a strong pan and to take care that it does not splash and become over-heated. If the sugar mixture is boiled to too high a temperature, it becomes dark in colour and bitter in flavour.

TO STORE BUTTERSCOTCH

Wrap individual sweets in waxed paper and store in an airtight container.

TO REHEAT BUTTERSCOTCH

Not to be recommended as it is difficult to reach the high temperature again and at the same time retain the good colour which is so much part of butterscotch. Reheating therefore is only recommended if a sugar thermometer is used.

Plain Butterscotch

450 g/1 lb granulated sugar
150 ml/¼ pint milk or double cream
3 tablespoons water
75 g/3 oz butter
pinch cream of tartar

Put the ingredients into a strong saucepan, stir over a low heat until the sugar has dissolved. Boil steadily, stirring once or twice, until the mixture reaches 'crack' stage or 138 c/280 f.

Lightly grease a 23-cm/9-in square tin with melted butter. Pour in the butterscotch; when nearly set, mark into squares. Leave in the tin until cold then wrap in waxed paper.

French Almond Rock

450 g/1 lb granulated or demerara sugar
225 ml/7½ fl oz water
50 g/2 oz glucose or ½ teaspoon cream of tartar
50 g/2 oz butter
175-225 g/6-8 oz almonds, blanched and split or flaked

Put the sugar, water and glucose or cream of tartar into a strong saucepan. Stir over a low heat until the sugar has dissolved. Boil, without stirring, until the mixture reaches 'light to hard crack' stage or 127-138 c/260-280 f. The temperature can be varied as to whether you like a hard or very hard sweetmeat. Add the butter and almonds; blend into the mixture.

Grease a 23-25-cm/9-10-in square tin with a little melted butter. Pour in the rock and allow to set. Break in pieces when cold and wrap in waxed paper.

VARIATION

This recipe can be used instead of the one on page 66 for Buttered Brazils and Buttered Walnuts. Use double the amount of nuts for the quantity of sweetmeat given above; follow the procedure for coating the nuts given on page 66.

Buttered Brazils or Walnuts

*While the recipe for Plain Butterscotch can be used, the
proportions below give a sweetmeat that is better for coating.*

15 Brazils or 18 walnuts
25 g/1 oz glucose, preferably liquid type
225 g/8 oz granulated or demerara sugar
scant 150 ml/¼ pint water
25 g/1 oz butter

Place the nuts on a flat plate or tin and position near the cooker so
they become slightly warmed. Put the glucose, sugar and water
into a strong saucepan, stir over a low heat until the sugar has
dissolved. Boil steadily until the mixture reaches 'hard crack' stage
or 138 c/280 f; add the nuts and butter and blend with the mixture.

Lightly grease a flat tin with melted butter or oil. Lift the nuts
out of the butterscotch, making quite certain they are thinly and
evenly coated with the mixture. Place on the tin, allow to set, then
wrap in waxed paper.

VARIATION

Almond Butterscotch: use 175-225 g/6-8 oz whole blanched almonds
instead of Brazils or walnuts.

Uncooked Toffee

225 g/8 oz golden syrup
225 g/8 oz dried milk powder, preferably full-cream
1-2 teaspoons vanilla essence

Put the ingredients into a large basin over a pan of hot water. Heat
only until the syrup has melted. Stir from time to time to blend the
milk powder with the syrup. Remove from the heat and cool
sufficiently to handle, then knead until smooth. Allow to cool but
before the mixture becomes firm cut into pieces with a pair of sharp
scissors or a knife.

Barley Sugar Sticks

450 g/1 lb granulated or loaf sugar
150 ml/¼ pint water
few drops saffron yellow colouring
½ tablespoon lemon juice

Put all the ingredients into a strong saucepan, stir over a moderate heat until the sugar has dissolved. Boil steadily, without stirring, until the mixture reaches 'brittle' stage or 156 c/312 f.

Grease a slab or tin with a *very little* oil or melted butter. Allow the mixture to cool a little so it becomes slightly sticky then pour on to the slab or tin. Leave until cool enough to handle, then pull into very long thin strips. Twist these into the familiar barley sugar sticks. Wrap in waxed paper.

VARIATIONS

Barley Sugar Sweets: use the recipe above but instead of twisting the sweet, pour into a 20-cm/8-in square oiled or buttered tin. Mark into neat pieces when half set.

Glucose Barley Sugar: follow the basic recipe above but use 225 g/8 oz sugar and 225 g/8 oz liquid glucose.

Lemon Barley Sugar: follow the recipe for Barley Sugar Sticks but add the thinly pared rind (use only the top yellow 'zest') of 1 large lemon to the sugar and water. Remove before 'brittle' stage is reached.

Toffee-Coated Sweetmeats

Choose fondant (as pages 74 to 76), nuts, caramels (as pages 45 to 49) or glacé cherries, and any toffee recipe.

Brush a flat tin with melted butter or oil. Turn the sweetmeats in the hot toffee until completely coated. Place on the tin; allow to set.

Edinburgh Rock

This old traditional Scottish sweetmeat is flavoured and tinted with various essences and culinary colourings; for example the following can be added: raspberry essence and pink colouring, lemon essence and saffron yellow colouring, or peppermint essence and green colouring. All the flavourings and colourings should be delicate and pale.

450 g/1 lb granulated or loaf sugar
200 ml/7 fl oz water
pinch cream of tartar
flavourings and colourings (see above)
To dust
little icing sugar

Put the sugar and water into a heavy saucepan, stir over a low heat until the sugar has dissolved. Boil steadily until the mixture reaches 'light crack' stage or 129 c/265 f; this is a little softer than butterscotch. Add the cream of tartar, stir well; allow to cool in the saucepan until the mixture thickens very slightly.

Brush two or three large flat tins with melted butter or oil; divide the sweetmeat into two or three portions and place each on a tin.

As soon as the sweetmeat is sufficiently cool to handle add the flavouring and colouring; knead until evenly blended into the mixture.

Dust the slab and your fingers with icing sugar and pull and knead each section of sweet until it becomes rather dull. When you have made really long thin sticks, cut into lengths of about 13 cm/5 in.

Leave at room temperature until the rock becomes quite powdery and soft. This will take up to a day in warm weather and even a little longer if the weather is cold. Store in boxes.

VARIATION

If you prefer a softer version of this traditional Scottish sweet, use 300 ml/$\frac{1}{2}$ pint water and $\frac{1}{4}$ teaspoon cream of tartar to the 450 g/1 lb sugar, with flavourings and colourings as above. This sweet is much affected by weather conditions; in cold weather you can boil to 121 c/250 f only, in hot weather to 127 c/260 f.

Boiled Sweets

These are extremely wholesome and because they are not rich in fats, this type of sweetmeat can be given to children; however care should be taken that a boiled sweet does not stick in the throat of a small child.

METHOD OF MAKING BOILED SWEETS
Since the term 'boiled sweets' covers a variety of different recipes, specific advice is given in individual recipes.

USE OF BOILED SWEETS
These are a complete sweetmeat and are not suitable for coating in chocolate.

DISADVANTAGES OF BOILED SWEETS
The mixture is quite difficult to make and to handle, since one has to work the very hot sugar mixture.

PROBLEMS OF MAKING BOILED SWEETS
Outlined in the point immediately above. It is essential to attain the recommended temperature.

TO STORE BOILED SWEETS
These do not need wrapping, unless specifically stated in the recipe. Keep in an airtight jar or tin.

TO REHEAT BOILED SWEETS
It is not advisable to try and reheat these, since the texture and colour could be spoiled.

Sugar Lollies

Children love a sugared sweet on a stick. Choose any of the boiled sweet recipes on the following pages. Allow the mixture to cook, as in the recipe, then to cool slightly, so it can be handled. Take out small amouts and mould these into rounds; insert a wooden stick, or the plastic type of stick used for iced lollies, into the mixture, then mould again to make a flattish round or oval shape. Wrap the sweetmeats in waxed paper so they do not get over-sticky.

Acid Drops

450 g/1 lb granulated or loaf sugar
150 ml/$\frac{1}{4}$ pint water
7 g/$\frac{1}{4}$ oz tartaric acid, sifted

Put the sugar and water into a strong saucepan, stir over a moderate heat until the sugar has dissolved. Boil steadily, without stirring, until the mixture reaches 'brittle' stage, or 156 c/312 f. During the boiling stage skim the mixture (i.e. remove any grey bubbles that rise to the top) for this scum will spoil the clarity of the sweetmeats.

Allow to cool slightly in the saucepan but while it is still of a pouring consistency, add the tartaric acid. Mix thoroughly.

There are two ways of shaping the sweetmeat:
a) Pour into individual *ungreased* tiny moulds and allow to set, or
b) Allow the mixture to cool until it can be handled then form into long bars and cut into individual portions.

Acid drops can be rolled in a little sifted icing sugar.

VARIATIONS

Fruit Drops: use the recipe for Acid Drops but work in a few drops of raspberry, lemon or orange essence with appropriate colourings, as well as the tartaric acid.

Fresh Fruit Drops: use the recipe for Acid Drops above, omit the tartaric acid. Instead of water use fresh apple, grapefruit, orange or pineapple juice. You can also use a smooth fruit purée, such as sieved cooked rhubarb, sieved uncooked raspberries or strawberries instead of the juice. This does not produce such a clear sweet, but the flavour is excellent. Diluted blackcurrant syrup could be used.

Ginger Drops: use ginger beer instead of water, or omit the tartaric acid and flavour the sweetmeat with a little ground ginger.

Peppermint Lemon Drops: use the recipe for Acid Drops but add a few drops of peppermint essence and green colouring.

Mint Humbugs

450 g/1 lb demerara sugar
150 ml/¼ pint water
50 g/2 oz butter
½-¾ teaspoon peppermint essence or a few drops oil of
peppermint
pinch cream of tartar

Put all the ingredients into a strong saucepan and stir over a low heat until the sugar has dissolved. Boil steadily, stirring once or twice, until the mixture reaches 'hard crack' stage, 143 c/290 f. Allow the mixture to cool a very little so it becomes slightly sticky.

Grease a slab or tin with a very little oil or melted butter. Pour the mixture on to the slab or tin, leave until cool enough to handle, then pull into long strips. When cold cut into small pieces. Store in an airtight tin.

VARIATIONS

Chewy Mint Humbugs: instead of 450 g/1 lb sugar in the recipe above, use 400 g/14 oz sugar and 50 g/2 oz golden syrup.

Lemon Humbugs: follow the recipe for Mint Humbugs but use granulated sugar and lemon essence instead of peppermint essence.

Orange Humbugs: follow the recipe for Mint Humbugs but use granulated sugar and orange essence; a few drops of orange colouring can be added.

Raspberry Humbugs: follow the recipe for Mint Humbugs but use granulated sugar and raspberry essence with pink colouring.

Shaded Mint Humbugs: use the recipe for Mint Humbugs but pull half the mixture rather more vigorously so it is a little paler in colour. Put the pale strip and the dark strip together and roll up so you have a slightly striped effect.

Harlequin Humbugs: omit the peppermint, make the sweetmeat and divide into three portions. Work various flavourings and colourings into each portion, pull these to form long strips then place these together for a striped effect. Cut into pieces.

Praline

This sweetmeat needs very much the same ingredients as candy. You could use the candy recipe given on page 36 as a change from the special praline recipes below and opposite.

Whichever recipe is used you must heat half, or all, the sugar or all the golden syrup first until it forms a golden caramel. This gives that characteristic flavour to the sweetmeat. If you caramelize only half the sugar you obtain a more delicate taste than when all the sugar has been turned into a caramel. Always allow the caramelized sugar or syrup to cool slightly before adding the other ingredients and blend these with the caramel over a low heat. This prevents any possibility of the mixture curdling.

Walnut Praline

450 g/1 lb granulated sugar
150 ml/¼ pint water
50 g/2 oz butter
1 teaspoon vanilla essence
175 g/6 oz walnuts, chopped

Put half the sugar and all the water into a strong saucepan. Stir over a moderate heat until the sugar has dissolved, then boil without stirring until a golden brown caramel, see page 17.

Allow the mixture to stand for 5 minutes then add the remaining sugar, the butter and vanilla. Stir over the heat until the second amount of sugar has dissolved, bring to the boil and cook until the mixture reaches 'soft ball' stage or 114-115 c/238-240 f. Grease a 20-cm/8-in square sandwich tin with butter. Add the walnuts to the praline. Pour the mixture into the buttered tin; allow to set and cut into pieces.

VARIATION

Golden Syrup Praline: use 100 g/4 oz golden syrup and 350 g/12 oz granulated sugar instead of all sugar. Allow the syrup to form a golden brown caramel, then proceed as above.

VARIATIONS ON WALNUT PRALINE

Follow the basic recipe opposite but make the following adaptations.

Chocolate Praline: omit the walnuts. Chop 100 g/4 oz plain chocolate into small pieces and add to the sweetmeat when the mixture reaches the 'soft ball' stage. Blend into the hot praline.

Chocolate Walnut Praline: either add the chocolate to the mixture as described above, or blend in 40 g/1½ oz cocoa powder or 75 g/3 oz chocolate powder when the mixture reaches boiling point after the second addition of sugar has dissolved.

Coconut Praline: omit the walnuts in the recipe opposite. Add 100-175 g/4-6 oz finely grated or shredded fresh coconut when the mixture reaches boiling point after the second addition of sugar has dissolved. The Golden Syrup Praline could be used with coconut.

Maple Praline: omit the golden syrup in the Golden Syrup Praline. Use maple syrup instead and heat this for a short time only; do not allow it to change colour, for this spoils the flavour.

Caramel for Decoration

Caramelled sugar can be used as a decoration on cakes or on top of sweetmeats, such as fondants. You can make caramel with castor, granulated or loaf sugar. To each 25 g/1 oz sugar allow 1 tablespoon water. Put the sugar and water into a strong saucepan, stir over a moderate heat until the sugar has dissolved, then stop stirring and allow the mixture to boil until it changes colour. As the table on pages 16 and 17 shows, there is a range of temperatures for caramel, ranging from 155.5 c/312 f upwards. The higher the temperature the darker the caramel.

Pour the caramel on to a lightly oiled tin, allow to set, then crush lightly with a rolling pin. Store in an airtight tin.

CHAPTER 3

SOFT AND DELICATE

This chapter covers a diversity of sweetmeats, all of which are delicate to the touch and soft on the palate. It starts with fondant and, while fondants may feel firm on the outside, they should be beautifully soft in the centre.

The next section is for jellied sweets of various kinds, including Marshmallows and Turkish Delight, pages 90, 91 and 92.

The final part of the chapter deals with spun sugar, ideally as delicate as a cobweb, and delicious crystallized fruits and flowers. The outside may be crisp, but good crystallized fruits should never lose their luscious juicy taste.

Fondants

Fondants are fairly firm sweets which, because of their almost pure sugar content, tend to be very sweet and keep well. You can make a large quantity of fondant, use the amount as required and store the rest.

METHODS OF MAKING FONDANT

Fondant can be made by blending icing sugar with egg white and flavouring, or by boiling together sugar, water and glucose.

Uncooked fondant is opposite and cooked fondant on page 76.

USE OF FONDANT

This can be used as a sweetmeat by itself as in the recipes that follow, or as a filling, see page 78. Various colourings and flavourings can be added to the melted fondant, or the softened fondant may be mixed with nuts or glacé fruits.

DISADVANTAGES OF FONDANT

Individual fondants can look amateur unless you use moulds or are skilled at moulding the mixture.

PROBLEMS OF MAKING FONDANT

It is essential to allow cooked fondant to reach the right temperature and to handle it as described in the recipes. Overbeating of the fondant mixture while it is being cooked may cause the grains to separate and you will then find it difficult to mould the fondant. The best result is obtained by kneading it on a slab, unless stated to the contrary.

TO STORE FONDANT

Fondant will harden with storing, even when put in foil or a tin, but this is no problem since it is so easily reheated. Wrap the fondant in waxed paper or foil, store in a covered tin in a cool place. It keeps for many weeks. Use as required.

TO REHEAT FONDANT

Take the required amount of fondant, put it into the top of a double saucepan or a basin placed over a pan of boiling water. Heat until it has melted. For coating, thin slightly, see page 80.

Uncooked Fondant 1

450 g/1 lb icing sugar, sifted
2 egg whites
½ tablespoon lemon juice
colouring and flavouring, as individual recipes

Put the ingredients into a basin and beat until a stiff smooth mixture. If the egg whites are rather small you may need a little extra lemon juice or water to give the correct consistency.

If using an electric mixer choose a low speed.

If using a food processor allow only about 25 seconds processing.

Add colouring and flavouring as in the individual recipes.

Note To make a softer fondant add 1-2 teaspoons glycerine or liquid glucose.

VARIATION

Uncooked Fondant 2: sift 450 g/1 lb icing sugar and blend it with approximately 5 tablespoons condensed (sweetened) canned milk; add this gradually to achieve the desired consistency. Add colouring and flavouring as desired. This is a softer and stickier fondant than the basic recipe above.

Cooked Fondant 1

450 g/1 lb granulated or loaf sugar
225 ml/7½ fl oz water
40 g/1½ oz glucose

Put the sugar and water into a strong saucepan, stir over a moderate heat until the sugar has dissolved, then add the glucose. Boil quickly until the mixture reaches 'soft ball' stage or 115-118 c/ 240-245 F. The higher temperature produces a slightly firmer mixture than the usual 'soft ball'.

The varying temperatures enable one to have the right degree of hardness for individual tastes and, if liked, fondant can be softened for fillings and coatings, see page 80.

Do not beat fondant in the pan otherwise it may become granular, but allow to cool and stiffen very slightly.

Sprinkle a little warm water on to a slab and turn the sweetmeat out of the saucepan; allow to stand for a few minutes to set a little and cool slightly before handling.

Work the fondant up and down with a spatula or palette knife until it becomes very white and firm in texture. It can be flavoured and coloured and used at once as individual recipes, or allowed to become quite cold, wrapped and stored.

VARIATIONS

Cooked Fondant 2: use 300 ml/½ pint water and 20 g/¾ oz glucose to the 450 g/1 lb sugar. Follow the instructions given for Cooked Fondant 1, above, but allow the mixture to boil only until it reaches 114 c/238 F (very slightly lower than that given for the basic recipe above). This produces a softer fondant, but one that is very versatile.

Cooked Fondant 3: use the same amount of sugar and water as in the basic recipe, but omit the glucose. Stir until the sugar has dissolved, then add 2 tablespoons golden syrup (do not exceed this amount). Allow the mixture to reach 'soft ball' stage, as in the basic recipe, or even a very slightly lower temperature, i.e. 114 c/238 F. This makes a fondant that is slightly sticky, and therefore very pleasant as a filling, but it is not a good fondant for moulding.

FLAVOURING FONDANT

The quantities given below refer to uncooked or cooked fondant based on 450 g/1 lb sugar, see pages 75 and 76.

Chocolate Fondant: there are two ways of giving a chocolate flavour to fondant, the best taste being achieved by method a).
a) Melt 100-175 g/4-6 oz plain chocolate with up to $\frac{1}{2}$ teaspoon vanilla essence in a basin over hot water; allow to cool until the mixture begins to thicken slightly. Blend with the fondant.
b) Sift 25 g/1 oz cocoa powder or 50 g/2 oz chocolate powder with the icing sugar in the uncooked fondant or add this to any of the cooked fondant recipes when it reaches the stage or temperature given in the recipe.

Coffee Fondant: add 2-3 teaspoons instant coffee powder to the sugar in any of the recipes or use strong black coffee in place of water in Cooked Fondant 1, 2 and 3.

Lemon Fondant: add a few drops of lemon colouring and lemon essence to the fondant, or add the very finely grated rind of $\frac{1}{2}$-1 lemon in Cooked Fondants 1, 2 and 3 and replace 2 tablespoons water with 2 tablespoons lemon juice.

Maple Syrup Fondant: use the ingredients in Cooked Fondant 3 but substitute maple syrup for golden syrup.

Orange Fondant: work a few drops of orange colouring and orange essence into the fondant or add the very finely grated rind of 1-2 oranges and use orange juice in place of water in Cooked Fondants 1, 2 and 3.

Raspberry or Strawberry Fondant: work a few drops of pink colouring and raspberry or strawberry essence into the fondant.

SIMPLE SWEETS FROM FONDANT

The quantities, where given, are based upon 450 g/1 lb icing sugar, as in recipes 1 and 2 on page 75, or on 450 g/1 lb sugar, as in the cooked fondant on page 76. The mixture can be made into balls, as suggested below, or cut into fancy shapes.

Almond Creams: add a few drops of almond essence and colouring to the fondant, roll into small balls, flatten and top with blanched almonds.

Cherry Balls: chop 100-175 g/4-6 oz glacé cherries, add to the fondant, mix thoroughly then roll into balls.

Cherry Coconut Balls: use the quantity of glacé cherries as above, roll into balls then roll in desiccated coconut.

Coconut Balls: add 50 g/2 oz desiccated coconut to the fondant, roll into balls then roll in desiccated coconut.

The coconut for the coating could be toasted until a golden brown before use.

Date Balls: chop 100 g/4 oz dates (weight when stoned); use as glacé cherries above.

Stuffed Dates: make the fondant a little softer than usual; this means using slightly more lemon juice in the uncooked fondant and adding a little double cream to the cooked fondant. A few blanched and chopped almonds can be added to the fondant. Slit dessert dates, remove stones and fill with fondant.

Ginger Balls: chop 100-175 g/4-6 oz glacé or well-drained preserved ginger. Mix a good pinch of ground ginger into the fondant together with the chopped ginger. Roll the mixture into balls.

Harlequin Shapes: cooked or uncooked fondant can provide a complete selection of sweetmeats if you add various colourings and flavouring to small batches of the mixture. Cut into fancy shapes, such as stars, hearts, diamonds etc.

Top the sweetmeats with silver balls, crystallized rose petals, angelica, glacé cherries and nuts.

Hazelnut Creams: use either Uncooked Fondant 1 or Cooked Fondant 1 or 2 on pages 75 and 76. Add a very little double cream to either mixture, with a few drops of raspberry essence and pink colouring.

If using rubber sweet moulds: put an unblanched hazelnut into each mould. Add the soft uncooked fondant or pour the hot cooked fondant over the nuts. Allow to set.

If moulding the sweets: allow cooked fondant to cool enough to handle. Knead as given below, form into rounded conical shapes, press a hazelnut in the top of each shape; mark the sides with vertical lines, using a fine needle. Allow to set.

Peppermint Creams: use either Uncooked Fondant 1 or 2 or Cooked Fondant 1 or 2 on pages 75 and 76. Work 2 teaspoons glycerine into the uncooked fondant to keep it fairly soft. Every type of fondant can have a little double cream added, but the mixture must be firm enough to roll out. Flavour the mixture with oil of peppermint or peppermint essence. Roll out to 5-mm/$\frac{1}{4}$-in thickness, cut into 2.5-cm/1-in rounds. Allow to set.

The mixture could be flavoured with crème de menthe liqueur, instead of peppermint, and tinted a pale green.

TO MOULD FONDANT

Although uncooked fondant could be used for Hazelnut Creams, cooked fondant is better for moulding larger shapes, such as the Sugar Mice on page 80. Knead the fondant until quite smooth, take off the required amount, knead again then shape. Dust your fingers with sifted icing sugar. If the fondant has to be rolled out, as for Peppermint Creams, then use plenty of sifted icing sugar on the board and rolling pin.

Sugar Mice

Cooked Fondant 1 or 2 (page 76)
fine string
Glacé Icing, (page 107)
colouring

Make the fondant as page 76.

METHOD 1: It is possible to buy tiny animal moulds which are normally used for jellies. These are perfectly satisfactory for making animal shapes in fondant. Since this hard sugar sweet sets quite firmly it should not be necessary to grease the mould. Simply press the warm fondant into the mould, put a tiny piece of string into the fondant for the tail. Allow the sweetmeat to set then turn out of the mould.

Make up a small amount of glacé icing and colour this. Pipe eyes, nose and mouth on the fondant shape.

METHOD 2: Mould the warm icing into oval shapes for the body and round shapes for the head. Insert a small piece of string into the body for the tail. Stick the heads on to the bodies with more warm fondant then mould the fondant to give the ears and nose for the mice. Decorate with glacé icing as above.

To Coat in Fondant

Cooked Fondants 1 or 2 can be used to coat nuts, crystallized fruits, shapes of marzipan or truffles.

Fondant 1 makes a rather firm coating, so it is advisable to thin this slightly. Cook the fondant, then to each 225 g/8 oz allow 1 tablespoon Sugar Syrup (see page 110) or $\frac{1}{2}$ tablespoon double cream. Use half these amounts with Cooked Fondant 2. Add colouring and flavouring as desired; stir until a thick pouring consistency. If the fondant has become too set reheat gently, as page 74.

Arrange the nuts or sweetmeats on a slab and spoon over the fondant, or pour a very little into rubber sweet moulds, add the nuts or sweetmeats then cover with more fondant.

Coconut Cream Fondant

Cooked Fondant 1 or 2 (page 76), made with 450 g/1 lb sugar
etc.
2 tablespoons double cream
175 g/6 oz desiccated coconut
pink colouring

Remove the saucepan of fondant from the heat when it reaches the stage or temperature in the recipe, add the cream, coconut and enough colouring to produce a pale pink sweetmeat. Grease an 18-20-cm/7-8-in square tin. Put in the mixture. Allow to cool then cut into squares.

VARIATIONS

If using fondant that has been stored, warm this in a basin over hot water until softened then add the ingredients as above. Uncooked fondant made with 450 g/1 lb icing sugar, as page 75, could be used for this sweetmeat.

Turkish Creams

100 g/4 oz blanched almonds
Cooked Fondant 2 or 3 (page 76), made with 450 g/1 lb sugar
etc.
2 tablespoons double cream
50 g/2 oz walnuts, chopped
50 g/2 oz dried figs, chopped
100 g/4 oz sultanas or seedless raisins
50 g/2 oz glacé cherries, chopped
50 g/2 oz glacé pineapple, chopped

Shred the almonds, place on a flat baking tray and brown under the grill or in a moderate oven (180 c, 350 f, gas 4), until golden.
Make the fondant as the recipes on page 76; when the mixture reaches the stage or temperature in the recipe, add the almonds, cream and remaining ingredients. Mix thoroughly. Turn on to a slab, knead well then form into small balls or cut into fancy shapes.

TO MAKE COCONUT ICE

This popular sweetmeat is based upon uncooked or cooked fondant, so the information given on pages 74 to 75 is extremely important.

Coconut Ice is inclined to become dry and crumble if kept for too long a period. It can then be used as a cake filling or decoration; break it into pieces and blend with whipped unsweetened cream or creamed butter.

The recipes including a little cream do not easily crumble.

The desiccated coconut in the uncooked or cooked Coconut Ice could be replaced with freshly grated coconut. Reduce the amount of liquid by 1 tablespoon in the Uncooked Coconut Ice on this page; eat the sweetmeat when fresh. In the cooked Coconut Ice opposite add the grated coconut when the sugar has dissolved then proceed as the recipe. The sweetmeat keeps well.

Uncooked Coconut Ice

5 tablespoons full-cream condensed (sweetened) canned milk
450 g/1 lb icing sugar, sifted
175 g/6 oz desiccated coconut
pink colouring

Mix together the condensed milk, all the icing sugar except 1 tablespoon, and the coconut. The mixture will be thick so should be mixed very vigorously. Remove half the mixture from the bowl; shape into a neat oblong. Add the colouring to the remaining mixture, blend well then shape into another oblong identical in shape to the first. Put on to the white oblong; press together firmly. Dust a flat tin with the remaining icing sugar. Place the coconut ice on this, leave until firm then cut into neat slices.

VARIATION

Cream Coconut Ice: use double cream in place of condensed milk.

Coconut Ice

450 g/1 lb granulated sugar
150 ml/¼ pint water
25 g/1 oz glucose or pinch cream of tartar
100 g/4 oz desiccated coconut
1 tablespoon double cream
pink colouring

Put the sugar and water into a strong saucepan, heat and stir until the sugar has dissolved, then add the glucose or cream of tartar. Boil quickly until the mixture reaches 'soft ball' stage or 114 c/238 f. Remove the pan from the heat, add the coconut and cream, blend with the very hot sugar mixture and beat until cloudy.

Grease a 15-18-cm/6-7-in square tin with a very little butter. Spoon half the hot mixture into the tin, spread flat. Tint the coconut ice in the saucepan a pale pink and spoon over the white layer. Allow to set then cut into slices.

VARIATIONS

Cherry Coconut Ice: chop 100 g/4 oz glacé cherries, add to the mixture just before it reaches 'soft ball' stage.

Chocolate Coconut Ice: blend 40 g/1½ oz sifted cocoa powder or 50-75 g/2-3 oz chocolate powder or 100 g/4 oz grated plain chocolate into the mixture before adding the coconut and cream.

Coconut Kisses: use the basic recipe for Coconut Ice or any of the variations. Shape into tiny heaps on a buttered slab; allow to cool and set then wrap in waxed paper.

Coffee Coconut Ice: use 150 ml/¼ pint strong black coffee instead of water in the basic recipe.

Creamy Coconut Ice: use 2 tablespoons cream instead of 1.

Harlequin Coconut Ice: chop 50 g/2 oz glacé cherries and 50 g/2 oz angelica; add to the mixture just before it reaches 'soft ball' stage.

Coconut Chips

275 g/10 oz fresh coconut without any brown skin
575 g/1¼ lb granulated sugar
150 ml/¼ pint plus 2 tablespoons water

Cut the coconut into long thin strips with a very sharp knife or the shredding device on a food processor or electric mixer. Put 450 g/1 lb of the sugar and the water into a strong saucepan. Heat and stir until the sugar has dissolved then allow the mixture to boil until it reaches a 'thick syrup' stage (slightly softer than 'soft ball' or 113 c/235 f). Remove the pan from the heat and stand in a container of cold water to prevent the syrup remaining at the temperature. Add the coconut and turn in the syrup with a metal spoon so each piece is well covered. Allow to stay in the syrup for 5-6 minutes.

Spread the remaining sugar on a flat tin, add the drained coconut and turn in the sugar until coated. Cool then store in an airtight tin.

Note Use the coconut immediately after cutting. If any syrup remains, store in a covered container and use again.

Jellied Coconut Ice

This has a more delicate texture than the previous recipe.

Put 450 g/1 lb loaf sugar, 4 tablespoons single cream and 3 tablespoons milk into a strong saucepan. Stir over a low heat until the sugar has dissolved. Boil steadily, stirring from time to time, until the mixture reaches 'soft ball' stage or 114 c/238 f.

Meanwhile measure 1 tablespoon milk into a basin, sprinkle 1 teaspoon gelatine on top, leave for a few minutes to soften, then blend into the hot sugar mixture, together with 150 g/5 oz desiccated coconut. Mix well, beat until cloudy then continue as Coconut Ice on page 83.

Clockwise, from top left: Turkish Delight, Coconut Ice, Stuffed Dates and Cherry Balls

Jellied Sweets

Sweetmeats such as marshmallows and Turkish delight are examples of jellied sweets. It is worthwhile making a good quantity since they keep well.

METHOD OF MAKING JELLIED SWEETS

Although these sound simple to make, a certain amount of sugar boiling is necessary and care should be taken to see that the temperature given in the recipes is reached. Gelatine varies in strength, but the well-known makes should give you the correct result if the amount in these recipes is used. Individual envelopes of powdered gelatine contain 3 teaspoons, i.e. 14.179 g/$\frac{1}{2}$ oz. Specific points about making the sweetmeats are given in the individual recipe.

USE OF JELLIED SWEETS

These are a sweetmeat in themselves or they can be coated with chocolate. They are generally too fragile to be coated with fondant.

DISADVANTAGES OF JELLIED SWEETS

There are no particular disadvantages. The jellied sweets will keep in good condition if well dredged in icing sugar. If coating in chocolate, make quite certain that the chocolate has become cold.

PROBLEMS OF MAKING JELLIED SWEETS

In some recipes there is rather lengthy stirring of the mixture; this is very essential and must not be overlooked.

TO STORE JELLIED SWEETS

Pack in layers in boxes or tins; each layer should be covered with plenty of sifted icing sugar.

TO REHEAT JELLIED SWEETS

These are not suitable for reheating.

Note The recipe for Turkish Delight 2 on page 92 does not contain gelatine, but the prolonged cooking of the cornflour mixture produces a clear jellied appearance.

Above: Apricot Coconut Truffles and Chocolate Rum Truffles;
Below: a selection of hand-made chocolates

Apple Squares

1 kg/2 lb good cooking apples
300 ml/$\frac{1}{2}$ pint water
granulated sugar (see method)
gelatine (see method)
lemon juice (see method)
To coat
25 g/1 oz icing sugar, sifted

Wash and slice the apples; do not peel or core if you intend to sieve the fruit. If using a liquidizer then the peel and cores must be removed. Simmer the fruit and water until soft. Sieve or liquidize and return to the saucepan. Cook gently, stirring from time to time, until a very stiff purée. Measure this and to each 600 ml/1 pint purée allow 450 g/1 lb sugar, 40 g/1$\frac{1}{2}$ oz powdered gelatine, $\frac{1}{2}$ tablespoon lemon juice and 2 tablespoons water.

Return the purée to the pan, add the sugar and stir over a low heat until dissolved. Boil steadily, stirring from time to time, until the mixture reaches 'very soft ball' stage or 113 c/236 f.

Soften the gelatine in the lemon juice and cold water, add to the sugar mixture and stir over a very low heat until the gelatine has dissolved.

Lightly oil a 20-cm/8-in square tin, pour in the mixture then allow to set. Cut into squares with a damp knife or kitchen scissors. Roll in the icing sugar.

VARIATIONS

Apple Nut Squares: chop 100 g/4 oz nuts, add to the apple mixture just before 'soft ball' stage is reached.

Apricot Squares: soak 225 g/8 oz dried apricots in 1.15 litres/2 pints cold water for 12 hours. Simmer the fruit in this water until soft, then proceed as Apple Squares above. 1-2 tablespoons apricot brandy could be added to each 600 ml/1 pint purée.

Apricot Almond Squares: chop 100 g/4 oz blanched almonds, add to the apricot mixture, see directly above, before the 'soft ball' stage is reached.

French Jellies

450 g/1 lb granulated or loaf sugar
225 ml/7½ fl oz water
¼ teaspoon citric acid or 2 tablespoons lemon juice
20 g/¾ oz powdered gelatine
flavouring (see method)
colouring (see method)
To coat
25 g/1 oz icing sugar, sifted

Put the sugar and 150 ml/¼ pint of the water into a strong saucepan and stir over a moderate heat until the sugar dissolves. Add the citric acid or lemon juice, boil until the mixture reaches 'soft ball' stage or 114 c/238 f.

Soften the gelatine in the remaining cold water, add to the mixture in the saucepan and boil for 2-3 minutes. Pour the mixture into heatproof small containers. Add various flavouring essences, lemon, orange, raspberry, rum etc.; colour the mixtures accordingly. Dampen small tins, pour in the mixtures and allow to set. Cut into squares with a damp knife or kitchen scissors and roll in the icing sugar.

VARIATIONS

Fruit Jellies: use undiluted fruit juice, such as grapefruit, orange or pineapple, instead of the water in the recipe above, or use diluted blackcurrant syrup. The citric acid or lemon juice can be omitted or reduced in quantity. Unfortunately the very high temperature to which the mixture is boiled does destroy the vitamin content, but the jellies taste delicious.

Ginger Jellies: use only half the amount of citric acid or lemon juice in the basic recipe; add 1 teaspoon ground ginger to the sugar. When the sweetmeat has reached 'soft ball' stage or 114 c/238 f, remove from the heat. Chop 100-175 g/4-6 oz preserved ginger very finely, blend into the hot sugar mixture, then proceed as the basic recipe.

Lemon Jellies: use ½ teaspoon citric acid or 4 tablespoons lemon juice in the basic recipe.

Marshmallows

275 g/10 oz loaf or granulated sugar
150 ml/¼ pint plus 4 tablespoons water
4 tablespoons orange flower water or 2 tablespoons lemon
juice
½ tablespoon glucose
20 g/¾ oz powdered gelatine
1 egg white
40 g/1½ oz icing sugar, sifted
To coat
25 g/1 oz icing sugar, sifted

Put the sugar, 150 ml/¼ pint of the water, the orange flower water or lemon juice and the glucose into a strong saucepan. Stir over a low heat until the sugar has melted. Boil steadily until the mixture reaches 'firm ball' stage or 127 c/260 f.

Meanwhile, put the remaining water into a basin, sprinkle the gelatine on top and stand over a pan of very hot water until the gelatine has dissolved. Blend the dissolved gelatine into the sugar mixture.

Whisk the egg white until stiff in a large heatproof basin, then pour the hot sugar and gelatine mixture on to the egg white. Beat vigorously until the mixture begins to stiffen.

Line the base and sides of a 20-cm/8-in square tin with waxed or greaseproof paper. Sprinkle about 25 g/1 oz of the icing sugar over the paper. Pour the marshmallow mixture into the tin. Cover with the remaining icing sugar, then waxed or greaseproof paper and a quite heavy weight; this needs to give even pressure over the entire surface of the sweetmeat.

Allow to cool then cut into neat pieces with kitchen scissors. Roll in the remaining icing sugar. Leave the marshmallows in the air for at least 24 hours until the outside hardens, then pack in an airtight container.

Note The mixture can be tinted if desired.

VARIATION

Raspberry Marshmallows: use sieved uncooked raspberry purée instead of water in the recipe above. Cooked apricot purée or uncooked strawberry purée also make delicious marshmallows.

Turkish Delight 1

A fairly quick recipe.

450 g/1 lb loaf sugar
300 ml/½ pint water
25 g/1 oz powdered gelatine
4 tablespoons lemon juice
½ teaspoon tartaric acid
pink colouring
To coat
25 g/1 oz icing sugar, sifted

Put the sugar and all the water except 4 tablespoons into a strong saucepan; stir over a low heat until the sugar has dissolved. Soften the gelatine in the remaining cold water, add to the sugar mixture and stir until the gelatine has dissolved. Boil steadily for 8 minutes, stirring all the time, then add the lemon juice and tartaric acid.

Dampen two 15-cm/6-in square tins; pour half the mixture into one tin. Tint the remaining mixture in the saucepan a delicate pink and pour into the second tin. Allow the mixtures to set; cut into squares with a damp knife or kitchen scissors and roll in the icing sugar.

VARIATION

Add a few drops of peppermint essence to the mixture and tint it pale green instead of pink. For a more luxurious sweet, omit 4 tablespoons water and use 4 tablespoons crème-de-menthe liqueur; colouring is then unnecessary. If preferred, use the full amount of water, omit the lemon juice and substitute the crème-de-menthe.

Chocolate Turkish Delight

To make larger portions of Turkish Delight, use the recipe on this or the next page. Pour the mixture into a number of small oblong, square or round moulds, or patty tins. Leave until firm, turn out and then coat with cooled melted chocolate.

Turkish Delight 2

450 g/1 lb sugar
900 ml/1½ pints water
¼ teaspoon tartaric acid
200 g/7 oz icing sugar, sifted
75 g/3 oz cornflour
2 tablespoons lemon juice
50 g/2 oz honey
pink colouring
To coat
25 g/1 oz icing sugar, sifted

This is a less easy sweetmeat than recipe 1 on page 91, but it produces a better taste. The cloudy cornflour mixture becomes clear with prolonged cooking.

Put the sugar and 150 ml/¼ pint of the water into a strong saucepan, stir over a low heat until the sugar has dissolved, then allow to boil steadily until 'soft ball' stage or 116 c/240 f; add the tartaric acid.

Blend the icing sugar and cornflour with the rest of the cold water and pour into a second saucepan. Bring to the boil, stirring all the time, and boil until the mixture thickens. Add the syrup from the first saucepan to the cornflour mixture, then add the lemon juice. Boil steadily for 25-30 minutes in an uncovered pan until the mixture is straw-coloured and clear; stir frequently during this time. Add the honey, stir well to blend.

Lightly oil two 18-cm/7-in square tins or brush with a very little butter. Pour half the mixture into one tin. Tint the remaining mixture pale pink and pour into the second tin. Allow the mixture to set then cut into squares and roll in the icing sugar.

VARIATION

Crème-de-Menthe 2: follow the recipe above and add a few drops of peppermint essence. Use green instead of pink colouring. For a more luxurious sweet, omit the lemon juice, add 6-8 tablespoons crème-de-menthe liqueur and omit this amount of water.

Spun Sugar

To spin a sugar mixture is a craft that requires practice, for it is a skilled operation. Spun sugar is used to decorate iced desserts and pastries. A slightly different sugar mixture, given on the next page, enables you to mould flower petals, small baskets or other shapes to hold petits-fours.
When spinning sugar you may well find some of the mixture falls on the floor, so cover this with clean kitchen paper. You can then gather up any of the sugar mixture that falls on the paper, put it back in the saucepan and reheat it.
Choose a dry day for spinning sugar so that the mixture stays crisp, and make sure there is no steam in the kitchen.

450 g/1 lb loaf sugar
225 ml/7½ fl oz water
5 drops acetic acid
pinch cream of tartar

Put the sugar and water into a strong saucepan and stir over a low heat until the sugar dissolves. In this particular recipe it is better to use loaf sugar – it gives a clearer syrup than granulated. Add the acetic acid (which helps to make the mixture crisp) and the cream of tartar. Boil the mixture until it reaches 154 c/310 f; this is a 'very hard crack', just lower than the temperature at which a sugar mixture begins to change colour for a caramel. It really is important to use a sugar thermometer so the correct temperature is reached, but not exceeded. Remove the pan from the heat and stand in a metal container of cold water for 2-3 minutes only, to cool the syrup a little.

Grease a rolling pin or large wooden spoon with a very little oil. Dip the prongs of a fork or the tip of a metal spoon into the sugar syrup; make sure there is only a very little syrup on the fork or spoon. If you are right-handed hold the fork or metal spoon in your left hand and the end of the rolling pin or bowl of the wooden spoon in your right hand; this gives a better control over the heavier objects. Keep the hands as far apart as possible.

Hold the fork or spoon slightly downwards until you see thin threads forming, then toss these threads towards the rolling pin or wooden spoon handle. The higher you hold the fork or metal

spoon and the greater the dis-
tance between these and the
rolling pin or wooden spoon, the
longer the threads will be.

At first you will find this quite
difficult to do, but after only a
short time it becomes relatively
easy. Remove the brittle threads
from the rolling pin or wooden
spoon handle; while warm they
can be slightly twisted to give a
cobweb effect. When quite cold
store in a tightly sealed container,
lined with kitchen paper.

Moulded Spun Sugar

It is probably more correct to use the term 'pulled sugar' when
moulding, for the mixture is first pulled then moulded with the
hands. While the preceding recipe could be used for this purpose,
the following ingredients give a more pliable mixture.

Put 450 g/1 lb loaf sugar, 75 g/3 oz glucose, 225 ml/7½ fl oz
water and a squeeze of lemon juice into a strong saucepan; stir and
boil to 154 c/310 f, as described under Spun Sugar. Cool for 2-3
minutes over cold water until the mixture thickens very slightly in
the saucepan, then turn it on to a lightly oiled slab. While the
mixture is too hot to handle work it with a strong palette knife. To
do this, insert the knife into the edges of the mixture and move
these towards the centre. As soon as the sugar mixture can be
handled, pull and stretch with your fingers until it becomes a clear
stiff paste, then take off small pieces and form these into the desired
shapes. Allow to harden and cool. Store as Spun Sugar.

Note The sugar mixture can be tinted and flavoured with a few
drops of culinary colouring and essence. Add this when the
mixture has reached 154 c/310 f.

Crystallized Fruits

Commercially crystallized fruits are prepared with specialist equipment which includes a sugar hydrometer to measure the density of the sugar syrup. It is, however, possible to achieve a good result at home without this equipment.
Choose perfect fruit; it should be firm and ripe but never over-ripe. Divide oranges or tangerines into segments, remove all white pith. De-seed grapes, keep whole; skin if wished. Peel and quarter, then core small ripe dessert pears; sprinkle the pears with a little lemon juice to preserve the colour. Poach apricots, plums or greengages in a little water until just soft but unbroken. Strain and use the water as part of the liquid in the recipe below.

450 g/1 lb prepared fruit
175 g/6 oz granulated sugar plus extra sugar (see method)
300 ml/$\frac{1}{2}$ pint water

STAGE 1. Place the fruit in a fairly shallow dish. Put the sugar and water into a saucepan, stir over a moderate heat until the sugar has dissolved. Pour the hot syrup over the fruit, cover the dish and leave for 24 hours.

STAGE 2. Carefully drain the syrup from the fruit. Pour the syrup into a saucepan, add a further 50 g/2 oz granulated sugar. Stir over a low heat until the sugar has dissolved, pour over the fruit. Cover and leave for 24 hours. Repeat Stage 2 three times. You have used 175 g/6 oz sugar plus four batches of 50 g/2 oz and taken five days.

STAGE 3. Pour the syrup back into the saucepan. Add 75 g/3 oz sugar, stir until dissolved; add the fruit, simmer for 3 minutes. Return fruit and syrup to the dish, cover and leave for 24 hours. Repeat Stage 3. The syrup should now be like very thick honey. If a little thin repeat Stage 3 again.

STAGE 4. Drain off any surplus syrup. Place the fruit on a wire cooling tray over a large tin to catch any drips. To give a slightly crisp outside, place the fruit (on the cooling tray) in a very cool oven (100 c, 200 f, gas $\frac{1}{4}$) with the door left slightly ajar; leave for 30-45 minutes or until crisp. Cool, put into sweetmeat cases and pack in boxes.

Crystallized Canned Fruit

If using fruit canned in natural juices, without sugar, then drain the liquid from the can and use this instead of water. Proceed as the basic recipe above.

If using fruit in a sweetened syrup, pour 300 ml/½ pint of this syrup into a saucepan, add 50 g/2 oz sugar, as given in Stage 2 on page 95; continue from there as the basic recipe.

Crystallized Peel

225 g/8 oz peel from oranges, tangerines, lemons or limes
water (see method)
7 g/¼ oz bicarbonate of soda
350 g/12 oz granulated sugar

Remove any excess white pith from the peel. Cut into large pieces. Boil 1.15 litres/2 pints water, add the bicarbonate of soda, pour into a mixing bowl and put in the peel; leave for 20 minutes. Drain and rinse the peel in cold water, put into a saucepan with fresh water to cover. Simmer gently in a covered saucepan until the peel is tender, drain again and place in a basin.

STAGE 1. Put 225 g/8 oz of the sugar with 300 ml/½ pint water into a saucepan. Stir over a low heat until the sugar has dissolved; pour the hot syrup over the peel and leave for 48 hours.

STAGE 2. Drain the syrup from the peel, put into a saucepan. Add the remaining sugar, stir over a low heat until dissolved. Put in the peel, simmer until transparent. Drain off the syrup and reserve.

STAGE 3. Place the peel on a wire cooling tray with a tin underneath and put in a very cool oven, as in Stage 4 for Crystallized Fruit (see page 95).

STAGE 4. Boil the reserved syrup until thick and cloudy. Dip each piece of peel in the syrup and leave this to dry and harden.

TO STORE CRYSTALLIZED PEEL

Keep the peel well covered, otherwise it becomes very hard and dry. It is a good idea to cut the peel into convenient sized pieces to use in cakes and puddings while it is still fresh.

Crystallized Angelica

Choose young and tender stalks. Cut the stalks into convenient lengths. Wash and dry then place in a large basin or mixing bowl. Dissolve 7 g/¼ oz kitchen salt in 2.25 litres/4 pints boiling water. Pour over the angelica. Leave for 10 minutes then pour away the salted water and rinse the angelica in cold water.

Place the angelica in a saucepan of boiling water and boil steadily for 5 minutes or until tender. Drain and scrape away the outer skin. The angelica is then ready to crystallize. Proceed in exactly the same way as for Crystallized Fruit on page 95.

Crystallized Flowers

flower petals (see method)
25 g/1 oz gum arabic
4 tablespoons triple strength rosewater
castor sugar (see method)

Flower petals suitable for crystallizing are roses, violets, primroses and any other flower of the primula family such as polyanthus; also the blossoms of plum, cherry, apple, pear (the ornamental as well as the fruiting variety), and heather. The non-edible flowers are those which come from bulbs; these are poisonous in many cases. Take care that the flowers are fresh and perfect; do not pick when the weather is wet or even damp. Do not gather the flowers until the gum arabic solution has been prepared.

Cover the gum arabic with the rosewater and leave for 24 hours to melt. When properly melted, paint each flower petal completely on both sides, using a fine paint brush. Then, holding each flower by its stem, sprinkle all over with castor sugar. Leave in a dry room until firm then store in an airtight container.

CHAPTER 4

CHOCOLATES AND TRUFFLES

This section gives recipes and suggestions for homemade chocolates and truffles. Do not attempt to make the chocolate for coating the various fillings at home; it is not an easy process since it requires the correct room temperature and atmosphere as well as the right ingredients. Concentrate on preparing professional-looking and interesting chocolates; to coat the various fillings, choose chocolate couverture (obtainable from first-class grocers) or, better still, use top quality plain or milk block chocolate.

TO MOULD CHOCOLATE

Melted chocolate can be used to form shapes quite easily. To make Easter eggs or animal or fancy shapes, you need to buy the special moulds; these should be brushed with *a very little* oil first. Melt the chocolate carefully, see Stage 3 on page 100.

Easter eggs: buy two special half egg shapes. Pour sufficient hot chocolate over the inside to give an even coating. Set in a cool place, but not in the cold of a refrigerator. Carefully remove the two shapes from the moulds. Melt a little more chocolate, brush this over the edges of the two chocolate shapes and press together gently, so forming a complete egg. Lift carefully on to a band of foil or kitchen paper, pin this around the egg, so applying gentle pressure. Leave until firm.

The eggs are then ready to decorate. Pipe with a little melted chocolate or Royal Icing, as the recipe on page 107.

To make small moulds: coat individual moulds or paper cases with melted chocolate; use a double or treble thickness of case to ensure a good shape for the chocolate. Proceed as for Easter eggs above. When firm, remove from the mould or paper. Larger cases make an interesting container for ice cream and the small ones can be filled with liquid fondant, soft marzipan or truffle mixture to make part of a selection of chocolates.

CHOOSING THE FILLINGS FOR CHOCOLATE

The most suitable centres for coating are:

Candy: as the recipes on pages 36 to 37; the less sweet flavours are better.

Caramels: every kind.

Cherries: either glacé or Maraschino.

Coconut Ice: the recipe containing cream on page 83 is the ideal choice, for it is less inclined to crumble when dipped into the hot chocolate.

Fondants: every kind.

Fudge: the less rich types are better.

Jellied Sweets: such as Turkish Delight. The chocolate for coating must be cool (although still in a liquid state) so it does not melt the gelatine. Turkish Delight 2 on page 92 would be the best choice.

Marzipan: made as any of the recipes. The mixture can be softened very slightly by adding a few drops of sherry or liqueur; this gives a more succulent filling. Any marzipan sweets could be used instead of plain marzipan.

Nougat: it is better not to coat this in rice paper but to pour the mixture into a lightly oiled tin to set.

Nuts: various kinds, either as individual nuts or clusters.

Toffees: choose the softer variety such as Golden or Everton Toffee, rather than the hard brittles.

Truffles: choose the firmer type of mixture, such as those on page 106.

DECORATIONS FOR CHOCOLATES

Have decorations readily available before making the chocolates, for the coating sets very rapidly, and nuts, crystallized flower petals (see page 97), and silver dragees, need to be pressed on to the half set chocolate. A simple decoration is made by swirling the half-set coating with a fine skewer or dipping fork to give an interesting effect. Glacé or Royal Icings (see page 107) could be used to pipe on chocolates or petits-fours, or use melted chocolate. In this case the chocolate coating must first be set firmly.

To Make Chocolates

centres (page 99)
decorations (page 99)
chocolate couverture or plain or milk block chocolate

STAGE 1. Assemble all the centres; the fondant, fudge, marzipan or other fillings should be cut into neat squares, oblongs or rounds, or formed into small balls. Do not make the filling too large. Place the centres on the table as close to the working area as possible. There should be the minimum delay between melting the chocolate and dipping the centres.

Ingredients for decoration should be available too.

STAGE 2. Cover tins with waxed paper, so any excess chocolate that falls on the paper can be collected and reheated. Have one or two dipping forks or ordinary forks available; these are for turning the centres in the liquid chocolate.

STAGE 3. Break the chocolate into pieces; chocolate couverture is very hard and will need cutting or coarsely grating.

To melt chocolate: put into a large ovenproof basin or mixing bowl and stand over a saucepan of very hot, but not boiling, water. Leave until *just* melted. *Do not over-heat.* (You can of course use a microwave cooker for this purpose.) Remove the bowl of chocolate from the heat as soon as possible; naturally the chocolate will stiffen as it cools and you may need to reheat it if coating a large number of fillings.

STAGE 4. Put the first centre into the hot liquid chocolate (jellied sweets based on gelatine must be coated in cool chocolate). Turn with the fork until the filling is completely coated.

STAGE 5. Lift the sweet out and hold it above the bowl for a few seconds so that excess chocolate drops back into the bowl. Place on the waxed paper on the tin; decorate at once unless using a piped decoration (see page 99). Repeat until all the fillings are coated.

STAGE 6. Leave the chocolates until firm; lift from the paper. If there is any excess chocolate coating around the base of each sweetmeat, cut this away with a sharp knife, melt it again and use. Either wrap the individual chocolates or put into small confectionery cases.

Truffles

Truffles make an excellent accompaniment to coffee at the end of a meal as well as being an interesting sweetmeat. If using as a filling for chocolate, omit the coating given in the various recipes; normally though this is essential to cover the soft and delicate mixture.

Although the recipes vary considerably, the method of making is similar. Press the ingredients together as firmly as possible; if the truffle mixture seems rather soft, chill it well before forming into balls. The size varies – you may prefer them a little larger than given. The suggested number is based upon each truffle weighing about 7 g/$\frac{1}{4}$ oz before coating.

In many recipes chocolate is an ingredient; this should be melted over hot water or in a microwave cooker, as explained opposite under Stage 3.

To coat the truffles, put the icing sugar, or other ingredients, on to a flat dish and gently turn the small balls in this. If preferred, put the coating into a greaseproof or polythene bag, drop in the small balls and shake until thickly coated. The amount of coating is a generous one but this is necessary.

Apricot Coconut Truffles

100 g/4 oz dried apricots
50 g/2 oz walnuts, or other nuts
50 g/2 oz desiccated coconut
25 g/1 oz icing sugar, sifted
grated rind of 1 orange
apricot brandy or orange juice (see method)
To coat
25 g/1 oz desiccated coconut

Mince the apricots and nuts or put into a food processor; switch on until finely chopped. Add the coconut, sugar, orange rind and sufficient brandy or juice to bind. Form into 30-36 small balls and coat in the coconut.

Apricot Chocolate Truffles

100 g/4 oz plain chocolate
100 g/4 oz dried apricots
40 g/1½ oz ground almonds
1 tablespoon sieved apricot jam
25 g/1 oz icing sugar, sifted
½ tablespoon apricot brandy
To coat
25 g/1 oz chocolate vermicelli

Melt the chocolate (see page 100). Mince the apricots or put into a food processor and switch on until a smooth purée. Mix all the ingredients together. Chill well, form into about 36 small balls and coat in the chocolate vermicelli.

Angostura Truffles

175 g/6 oz plain chocolate
¼-¾ teaspoon angostura bitters
3 egg yolks · 75 g/3 oz butter
75 g/3 oz icing sugar, sifted
To coat
25 g/1 oz cocoa powder, sifted
25 g/1 oz desiccated coconut
25 g/1 oz icing sugar, sifted

Break the chocolate into pieces, melt (see page 100) and cool slightly. Add the angostura bitters and egg yolks to the hot chocolate; mix well. Place back over hot water and whisk until thick and creamy. Cream the butter and icing sugar until soft, then gradually blend in the chocolate mixture. Chill well then form into 40 small balls.

Blend the cocoa powder, coconut and icing sugar and use to coat the balls. They are very soft, so must be well coated.

From the top: Popcorn, Nougat and Marzipan Squares, Marzipan Fruits, Sugared Almonds

Cherry Truffles

50 g/2 oz icing sugar, sifted
50 g/2 oz cocoa or chocolate powder, sifted
100 g/4 oz fine plain cake crumbs
4 tablespoons sieved apricot jam
2 teaspoons apricot brandy
24 glacé cherries

Put half the icing sugar and half the cocoa or chocolate powder into a bowl, add the cake crumbs, apricot jam and brandy and mix well. Divide into 24 portions and mould around the cherries.

Mix the remaining icing sugar and cocoa or chocolate powder together and use to coat the truffles.

Note The cocoa powder makes a very strongly flavoured mixture.

VARIATION
Coat in chocolate vermicelli.

Cream Truffles

50 g/2 oz mixed dried fruit
4 tablespoons double cream
few drops vanilla essence
75 g/3 oz icing sugar, sifted
40 g/1½ oz chocolate powder
75 g/3 oz fine plain cake or sweet plain biscuit crumbs
To coat
50 g/2 oz chocolate vermicelli or plain chocolate, finely grated

Chop the dried fruit into smaller pieces with kitchen scissors. Whip the cream until just stiff then blend with the vanilla essence, icing sugar, chopped fruit, chocolate powder and crumbs. Form into about 40 small balls and roll in the chocolate vermicelli or grated chocolate. Chill well.

Above, clockwise from the top: Coconut Whispers, Brandy Snaps, Almond Petits-Fours;
Below: Caramelled Fruits

Chocolate Rum Truffles

100 g/4 oz plain chocolate
3 tablespoons condensed (sweetened) canned milk
2 teaspoons rum
75 g/3 oz fine plain cake crumbs
To coat
25 g/1 oz icing sugar, sifted
25 g/1 oz chocolate powder

Melt the chocolate (see page 100), add the condensed milk and rum. Allow to cool until the mixture becomes slightly sticky. Put in the cake crumbs; mix thoroughly. Form into approximately 30 small balls. Blend the icing sugar and chocolate powder and use to coat the truffles.

VARIATIONS

Use full-cream dried milk powder instead of cake crumbs. Chop 25 g/1 oz glacé cherries and add to the mixture with the crumbs.

Rum and Almond Truffles: use 75 g/3 oz made marzipan instead of cake crumbs. Work the rum into the marzipan then blend with the melted chocolate and only 1½ tablespoons condensed milk.

The rum could be omitted and the mixture flavoured with a few drops of almond essence and 2 teaspoons sweet sherry.

Honey Almond Truffles: omit the condensed milk in the recipe above, add instead 2 tablespoons thick honey, together with 50 g/2 oz very finely chopped blanched almonds. The truffles can be coated as in the recipe above, or use chocolate vermicelli or toasted chopped blanched almonds.

Frosted Fruits

These make delicious petits-fours or a contrast to dark truffles. Brush grapes, black, red or white currants with lightly whisked egg white. Coat in castor or sifted icing sugar. Allow to dry for several hours, but eat the same day.

Mixed Fruit Truffles

75 g/3 oz dried apricots
50 g/2 oz dates, weight without stones
75 g/3 oz dried figs
75 g/3 oz raisins
50 g/2 oz mixed nuts
50 g/2 oz mixed crystallized peel
50 g/2 oz desiccated coconut
To coat
50 g/2 oz desiccated coconut
25 g/1 oz icing sugar, sifted

Finely mince all the truffle ingredients, except the desiccated coconut, or put into a food processor and switch on until a sticky purée. Add the coconut. Form into about 60 small balls, oblongs or finger shapes.

Blend the coconut for coating with the icing sugar and roll the balls in this mixture.

VARIATION

Omit the dried figs and use glacé cherries instead.
The mixture can be flavoured with a very little rum or brandy.

Icings

A small amount of icing enhances the appearance of chocolates and petits-fours. Glacé or Water Icing can be used only to make simple line designs. Select Royal Icing to pipe small flower shapes or borders; colour as desired.

Glacé or Water Icing: sift 225 g/8 oz icing sugar, blend with a little water and flavouring essence of lemon or orange juice.

Royal Icing: lightly whisk 1 egg white, sift 225 g/8 oz icing sugar into the egg white, add 1 teaspoon lemon juice. Beat until smooth and shiny.

Raspberry Noyeau 2

225 g/8 oz Madeira or sponge cake, made into fine crumbs
100 g/4 oz castor sugar
4 tablespoons raspberry jam
few drops raspberry essence
100 g/4 oz almonds, blanched and chopped
2 tablespoons lemon juice
2 teaspoons sweet sherry
pink colouring
To coat
rice paper

Put all the ingredients, except the colouring, into a strong saucepan and stir over a low heat until the sugar has dissolved. Cook very slowly for 20 minutes, or until the mixture is very thick; stir continually so the mixture does not burn. Add a little colouring.

Line an 18-cm/7-in square tin with rice paper, add the noyeau mixture, cover with more rice paper. Put a light weight over the top and leave until cold, then cut into neat bars.

VARIATIONS

Almond Noyeau: use the recipe above for Raspberry Noyeau 2. Omit the raspberry essence, colouring and raspberry jam. Substitute almond essence and sieved apricot jam.

Cherry Noyeau: in recipe 1 (see page 42), increase the cherries to 100 g/4 oz; in recipe 2, use cherry jam instead of raspberry jam and cherry brandy in place of sherry.

Strawberry Noyeau: use strawberry essence rather than raspberry essence in recipes 1 (see page 42) and 2. Substitute sieved strawberry jam for raspberry jam in recipe 2.

Chocolate Noyeau Truffles: allow the mixture to become completely set and firm. Cut into squares. Melt 225 g/8 oz plain chocolate. Carefully coat each noyeau square in chocolate; allow the chocolate to become lightly set then roll in chocolate vermicelli.

CHAPTER 5

MARZIPAN, NUTS AND POPCORN

Marzipan is an invaluable sweetmeat as well as a popular icing. It can be used as a filling in chocolates; it can be mixed with chopped glacé fruits and/or nuts and formed into small fingers or balls.

Throughout this book there are many recipes based upon nuts, for these are an important ingredient in many kinds of caramel, toffee and other sweetmeats, including Nut Brittles on pages 62 and 63. In this section are classic recipes that include sugared almonds, luxurious marrons glacés and savoury salted nuts.

The section ends on page 117 with advice on preparing popcorn and ways of using this.

Cooked Marzipan or Almond Paste

225 g/8 oz granulated or loaf sugar
150 ml/$\frac{1}{4}$ pint water
pinch cream of tartar
175 g/6 oz ground almonds
few drops ratafia or almond essence
1 egg white
25 g/1 oz icing sugar, sifted

This marzipan is white and firm and excellent for moulding. The mixture is based upon a fondant so the advice given on pages 74 to 75 is important. Put the sugar and water into a strong saucepan and stir over a low heat until the sugar has dissolved. Add the cream of tartar and boil until the mixture reaches 'soft ball' stage or 116 c/240 f. Remove from the heat and beat until the mixture begins to turn cloudy, then add the ground almonds and essence.

Whisk the egg white until frothy, add to the ground almond mixture and stir over a very low heat for 2 minutes. Turn out of the pan on to a board dusted with the icing sugar. Allow to cool, knead lightly then use or wrap and store.

Uncooked Marzipan or Almond Paste

225 g/8 oz ground almonds
100 g/4 oz castor sugar
100 g/4 oz icing sugar, sifted
few drops ratafia or almond essence
2 small or 1 large egg yolk(s)

This is the classic uncooked mixture, used to coat cakes, as well as being a sweetmeat; it has an excellent flavour and is not too sweet.
Mix all the ingredients together; knead lightly and use.

VARIATIONS

Use slightly less egg yolk and add sweet or dry sherry or a liqueur to bind. Delicious for the centre of chocolates.

To give a lighter colour to the marzipan, which makes it ideal for tinting to form into flowers or fruits, bind the mixture with egg whites rather than egg yolks.

Economical Marzipan: this uses less of the expensive ground almonds and makes a marzipan that is easy to handle. Blend together 450 g/1 lb sifted icing sugar, 225 g/8 oz ground almonds, a few drops of almond or ratafia essence and 1 teaspoon liquid glucose. Bind with 1½-2 whole eggs or use just egg yolks or egg whites, if preferred.

Sugar Syrup

This is useful to store for thinning down fondants, marzipan centres, etc. It keeps for a long time, store as below.

450 g/1 lb loaf or granulated sugar
150 ml/¼ pint plus 4 tablespoons water

Put sugar and water into a pan. Stir over a low heat until the sugar dissolves, then boil rapidly until the mixture forms a syrup, 93 c/200 f. Strain carefully and store in screw-topped bottles.

Marzipan Fruits

A box of marzipan fruits looks most attractive. These are not difficult to make; tint and mould the marzipan. Dust the board and your fingers with a little sifted icing or castor sugar, so the marzipan does not become sticky. The easiest fruits are:

Apples: colour the marzipan a pleasant apple green and form into the shape of tiny apples. Dip a very fine brush into pink colouring and shade outside to look like a ripening apple. Press a clove into the base and a tiny angelica stalk into the top.

Bananas: colour the marzipan yellow like a banana. Form into tiny banana shapes. Dip a fine paint brush into either strongish coffee or rather thin diluted chocolate and brush on the brown marks of a banana.

Peaches: colour the marzipan a pinky yellow. Form into balls and then make into peach shapes. Dip a fine brush into the pink colouring and shade like a peach.

Pears: colour the marzipan a pleasant green and form into the shape of tiny pears. Dip a very fine brush into pink colouring and shade outside to look like a ripening pear. Press a clove into the base and tiny angelica stalk into the top.

Strawberries: colour the marzipan a very delicate pinky red with cochineal and 2-3 drops of saffron yellow so it is not too mauvy-red in colour. Form into strawberry shapes and top with tiny green marzipan stalks and/or leaf shapes. Make tiny indentations with a fine needle on the strawberries and dip in sugar.

VARIATIONS

Form the marzipan into small animal or flower shapes, or: *Acorns*: tint the marzipan a pale coffee colour, make acorn shapes; dip the base in melted chocolate or sieved apricot jam then chocolate vermicelli. *Carrots*: tint the marzipan orange, form into carrot shapes, top with green marzipan or angelica stalks. *Potatoes*: flavour the marzipan with chocolate powder and a little rum. Form into potato shapes, mark the 'eye' with a needle, roll in chocolate powder.

TO COAT IN MARZIPAN

Simple and delicious sweetmeats can be made by coating stoned dates, whole nuts, Maraschino cherries, squares of fudge and portions of glacé fruits, such as apricots, in marzipan. Divide the marzipan mixture into small pieces; to give a slightly crunchy texture, blend with a little castor sugar. Press out to a sufficiently large size to mould around the filling.

The combination of nougat and marzipan below makes a particularly pleasant sweetmeat.

Nougat and Marzipan Squares

450 g/1 lb granulated sugar
$\frac{1}{2}$ teaspoon glycerine
1 tablespoon lemon juice
175 g/6 oz almonds, blanched and chopped
175 g/6 oz glacé cherries, chopped
marzipan, made with 225 g/8 oz ground almonds etc. (page 110)
To coat
25-50 g/1-2 oz castor sugar

This is another chewy type of sweet, not as light as a true nougat. Put the sugar, glycerine and lemon juice into a strong saucepan, stir over a low heat until the suar has dissolved then allow the mixture to boil until it reaches 'firm ball' stage or 121 c/250 f. Add the almonds and cherries and mix well.

Grease a Swiss roll tin measuring approximately 15 × 25 cm/ 6 × 10 in with a little butter. Pour in the mixture, allow to become nearly set then mark into 2.5-cm/1-in squares; leave in the tin until cold.

When the sweetmeat is cold, roll out the marzipan until about 5 mm/$\frac{1}{4}$ in. in thickness; cut into 2.5-cm/1-in wide strips, then into pieces sufficiently long to enclose the nougat. Wrap the marzipan round the nougat squares, seal firmly and roll in castor sugar.

EASY SWEETS WITH MARZIPAN

Use either the uncooked or cooked marzipan on pages 109 and 110. The uncooked marzipan is easier to handle since it does not harden as quickly as the cooked variety.

Marzipan Fudge: make any of the fudge recipes in the section from page 20 to 31. Make marzipan with 225 g/8 oz ground almonds etc. The marzipan using equal quantities of ground almonds and sugar is a good choice for this recipe, since it is not too sweet. Roll out the marzipan to fit a fairly deep and lightly oiled 20-cm/8-in tin, top with the fudge, allow to set then cut into squares or fingers. The two delicate sweetmeats blend well.

Neapolitan Bars: divide the marzipan into three or four portions. Tint each portion a different colour. Roll out to equal-sized rectangles, then place one portion on top of another until you have three or four layers. Cut into small fingers and roll in castor or granulated or sifted icing sugar while still soft.

Stuffed Fruits: remove the stones from dates or lightly cooked prunes and fill with marzipan.

Chocolate Nut Clusters

To make perfectly shaped clusters you need to shape the nut and chocolate mixture while it is soft and pliable.

Melt the chocolate as described in Stage 3 on page 100. Add the nuts: these can be whole peanuts, but blanched almonds should be cut into strips (flaked almonds are too thin to make good clusters); Brazils, cashew nuts and walnuts should be cut into fairly large pieces. Blend the nuts with the chocolate; you can use up to 175 g/6 oz nuts to each 225 g/8 oz chocolate. Take small spoonfuls of the soft mixture, put in little heaps on a lightly oiled tin. Take a clean knife to shape each heap into a slightly neater round. Allow to set.

Sugared Almonds

It is not easy to make home-cooked sugared almonds look as professional as those you buy, but these are pleasant to eat.

175 g/6 oz large almonds, blanched
450 g/1 lb loaf sugar
150 ml/¼ pint water
pinch cream of tartar
colouring (optional)

After blanching the almonds dry them well, either by placing in a cool oven for a few minutes or by patting dry with kitchen paper. Arrange the nuts in a single flat layer in a flameproof container and keep warm near the cooker. Cover the container.

Put the sugar, water and cream of tartar into a strong saucepan, stir over a low heat until the sugar has dissolved. Boil until the mixture reaches a firm 'soft ball', 116 c/240 f. Check the mixture carefully – if there is any scum on top remove this. Tint the sweet mixture if desired. Pour some of the very hot sugar mixture over the nuts, turn these in the mixture with two spoons or flat-bladed knives. Allow this layer to set. Re-boil the sugar mixture in the saucepan to the right stage again; add a second coating to the nuts. Allow to set once more (each coating takes about 10 minutes to set). Continue like this until the nuts are thickly coated and all the sugar mixture is used. Store in an airtight container.

VARIATIONS

Fondant Almonds: mould soft uncooked or cooked fondant around the blanched almonds (or other nuts), see pages 75 and 76.

Caramelled Almonds: blanch 175 g/6 oz almonds. Put 175 g/6 oz granulated sugar, 40 g/1½ oz unsalted butter and ¼ teaspoon almond essence into a strong saucepan. Stir over a low heat until the sugar has dissolved. Boil to 'caramel' stage or 171 c/340 f. Add the nuts and coat in the mixture. Tip on to a flat tin. Allow to set then break into clusters. Store in an airtight container.

Marrons Glacés

Choose the chestnuts carefully; they must be perfect and fresh, so the flesh is pleasantly moist. Larger nuts are better.

1 kg/2 lb chestnuts
water (see method)
few drops vanilla essence
For the two syrups
675 g/1½ lb granulated or loaf sugar
600 ml/1 pint water
cream of tartar (see method)
vanilla essence (see method)

STAGE 1. Wash the chestnuts in cold water, slit the skins; take care that the nuts are undamaged. Put into boiling water, simmer for 5 minutes only. Remove from the liquid, cool only sufficiently to handle – the warmer the nuts, the easier it is to remove shells and skins. Remove the outer shells, then pull or scrape away the brown skin. Fill the pan with fresh cold water, add a few drops of vanilla essence. Simmer the nuts for about 15 minutes or until soft but unbroken. Test carefully, for the nuts will break if too soft, but they will not soften further after coating with the sugar mixture.

STAGE 2. Put 225 g/8 oz of the sugar, 400 ml/13 fl oz of the water, a pinch of cream of tartar and a few drops of vanilla essence into a strong saucepan; stir over a low heat until the sugar has dissolved. Boil only until a thin syrup, 104 c/220 f. Add the chestnuts, boil steadily in the syrup for *one minute only* then carefully pour into a heatproof bowl. Cover and leave the nuts soaking in the syrup for 48 hours. After this time lift the nuts from this syrup, which is not used again. (It is excellent as the basis for a fruit salad.)

STAGE 3. Put the remaining 450 g/1 lb sugar and 200 ml/6.5 fl oz water into the saucepan, add a pinch of cream of tartar and ½-1 teaspoon vanilla essence. Stir over a low heat until the sugar has dissolved, then boil until 'firm ball' stage, or 121 c/250 f. Remove from the heat, immediately add the chestnuts, turn gently and carefully in the sugar mixture until thickly coated.

STAGE 4. Place the nuts on a wire cooling tray, with a dish underneath to catch any drips; allow to dry out at room temperature. Put into paper cases and store in a covered container.

Salted Nuts

These are invaluable as a party 'nibble' and are easily prepared at home. The first recipe will suit people who are anxious to avoid extra fat in their diets, but the variation with butter or oil is richer.

selection of nuts, blanched as page 15 (see method)
best quality kitchen salt (see method)

Brazils and dried walnuts do not need skinning. Fresh walnuts should be skinned. Dry the nuts well if they have been blanched in water. Arrange each kind of nut on a separate flat baking tray or tin. Use good solid tins, so the nuts do not scorch, and have one flat layer. Sprinkle with salt. Allow approximately 1 teaspoon salt to each 450 g/1 lb prepared nuts.

Place in the centre of a moderate to moderately hot oven (180-190 c, 350-375 f, gas 4-5) and leave for about 20 minutes. Turn two or three times during the process so the nuts are well coated. Cool then store in airtight containers.

VARIATIONS

Buttered Salted Nuts: prepare the nuts. To each 450 g/1 lb prepared nuts allow 40 g/1½ oz butter or 1½ tablespoons oil. Heat the butter or oil in a large frying pan, toss the nuts in this until very well coated. Drain on kitchen paper, then toss in salt (allow 1 teaspoon to each 450 g/1 lb nuts). To give a better coating, place the salted nuts on to flat baking trays and heat in the oven, as above. Allow barely 15 minutes at the higher setting.

Spiced Nuts: use the basic recipe or variation above. Add about ½ teaspoon mixed spice or allspice to the salt.

TO STORE SALTED NUTS

Salted nuts should be stored in airtight containers. This makes certain the nuts do not become dry and wrinkled and that the salted coating does not become damp.

Popcorn

To 'pop' corn is a more interesting occupation for children, for it is impressive to hear and see the way the corn opens up and becomes crisp. An adult should supervise the procedure though, for the saucepan and corn get very hot.

15 g/½ oz butter
1 small can popcorn

Put the butter into a large heavy saucepan which has a well-fitting lid. Place the pan over a low heat and allow the butter to melt. Remove from the heat and add enough popcorn to give a single layer. Place the lid on the pan. Put over a moderate heat and wait for 3-4 minutes; during this time you will hear the sound of the corn popping. Do not lift the lid, otherwise the hot corn will leap from the pan. When all the corn has popped, lift the lid. The popcorn is ready to eat when it has cooled down slightly. It can, however, be used in a number of different ways. Popcorn softens very quickly with exposure to the air, so pop small amounts only.

WAYS TO USE POPCORN

Popcorn makes a good salted 'nibble'. Toss the warm popped corn in a very little butter, then in salt; or simply toss in salt.

Caramelled Popcorn: follow the recipe for Caramelled Almonds, page 114; use 600 ml/1 pint crisp popcorn instead of nuts.

Chocolate Popcorn: blend the cold crisp popcorn with melted chocolate. Allow 225-350 g/8 12 oz chocolate to 600 ml/1 pint popcorn. Put in clusters on to a lightly greased baking tray and allow to set.

Popcorn Toffee: make any of the toffee recipes on pages 53 to 58. Blend about 600 ml/1 pint cold crisp popcorn with the hot toffee mixture, then proceed as the recipe.

Caramel mixtures, given on page 45 to 49, could be used instead of toffee. Popcorn can take the place of nuts.

CHAPTER 6

PETITS-FOURS

A number of sweetmeats in this book make excellent petits-fours; especially Crystallized Fruits, Truffles, Turkish Delight and those made with marzipan. In this section are baked petits-fours that mix well with these sweetmeats and which can be stored in an airtight container or a freezer.

Coconut Whispers

1 (397-g/14-oz) can full-cream condensed (sweetened) milk
250 g/9 oz desiccated coconut
colouring (see method)
instant coffee powder or essence (see method, optional)
rice paper

Mix the condensed milk and coconut together. Separate into several batches if you want to use colouring; tint one batch pale pink, another pale green, keep one white and flavour another with a little instant coffee powder or essence, see below.

Put rice paper on to flat baking trays. Form about 50 miniature pyramids or 2.5-cm/1-in rounds on the rice paper with damp, but not wet, fingers. Bake in the centre of a moderate oven (160-180 c, 325-350 f, gas 3-4) for about 6 minutes, until just tipped with golden brown. Tear or cut round the rice paper. These tend to dry out and become less palatable, even when stored in an airtight tin. They freeze well; use within 6 months.

VARIATIONS

Chocolate Coconut Whispers: use about 25 g/1 oz less coconut and add 25 g/1 oz chocolate powder. These can be coated with melted chocolate when baked and cooled.

Coffee Coconut Whispers: omit 1-2 teaspoons coconut and use that amount of instant coffee powder; blend with the condensed milk before adding the coconut. If more convenient, use $\frac{1}{2}$ tablespoon coffee essence and about 1 extra tablespoon coconut.

Almond Petits-Fours

50 g/2 oz butter
100 g/4 oz castor sugar
50 g/2 oz icing sugar, sifted
few drops almond or ratafia essence
1 egg yolk
50 g/2 oz self-raising flour, or plain flour with $\frac{1}{2}$ teaspoon
baking powder
100 g/4 oz ground almonds
little extra castor sugar (optional)
little sherry or milk (optional)
To glaze
1 egg white
To decorate
glacé cherries, angelica, nuts

Cream the butter with the castor and icing sugars and essence. Beat in the egg yolk. Sift the flour, or flour and baking powder, with the ground almonds into the creamed mixture. Blend well.

To make biscuit shapes: knead the mixture until it binds together; roll out to a generous 5-mm/$\frac{1}{4}$-in thickness on a lightly sugared board. Cut into 2.5-cm/1-in rounds, diamonds, hearts and other shapes. Put on lightly greased baking trays.

To make piped shapes: add sufficient sherry or milk to make a firm piping consistency. Put the mixture into a large piping bag with a 5-mm/$\frac{1}{4}$ in pipe. Pipe out small shapes on to the lightly greased baking trays.

Brush the petits-fours with a little egg white. Top with small pieces of cherry, angelica or nut. Bake in the centre of a moderate oven (160 c, 325 f, gas 3) for 12-15 minutes. Cool on the baking trays for a short time then remove to a wire cooling tray. Store in airtight containers or freeze for up to 6 months. The mixture makes about 60 petits-fours.

VARIATION

Economical Almond Petits-Fours: instead of all ground almonds use half ground almonds and half very fine semolina or ground rice with slightly more almond essence. The mixture can still be piped providing the semolina *is* fine.

Brandy Snaps

Tiny versions of this biscuit can be made for petits-fours.

50 g/2 oz plain flour
50 g/2 oz butter or margarine
50 g/2 oz golden syrup
50 g/2 oz castor sugar
1 teaspoon brandy

Grease several flat baking trays as the biscuits spread out very much in baking. Grease the handles of one or two very thin wooden spoons, or use wooden skewers.

Sift the flour. Put the butter or margarine, golden syrup and sugar into a saucepan, heat only until the ingredients have dissolved. Add the brandy then the flour; stir to blend.

Put $\frac{1}{4}$-$\frac{1}{2}$ teaspoon of the mixture on to the trays; allow at least 5 cm/2 in space around each little biscuit. Place the first tray above the centre of a heated moderate oven (180 c, 350 f, gas 4) and bake for 6-7 minutes, until the biscuits are golden brown. Allow to cool for 1-2 minutes or until the first biscuit can be removed with a palette knife. Press quickly around the wooden spoon handle or skewer to give a curl. Hold for a few seconds then place on to a wire cooling tray. Continue like this. If by chance the biscuits harden on the baking tray, return to the oven for a minute to soften. It is advisable to bake one tray of biscuits at a time.

Always store in a completely airtight container apart from all other biscuits. Makes approximately 30.

VARIATION

Parisienne Biscuits: these are like a Florentine and easily made. Blanch and very finely shred 25 g/1 oz almonds, chop 25 g/1 oz glacé cherries and 25 g/1 oz crystallized peel into very small pieces. Prepare the biscuit mixture but omit the brandy.

Cook the biscuits for 4-5 minutes or until well spread out, see above, then top with the nuts, cherries and peel; continue baking for 2-3 minutes. Lift off the baking trays and allow to cool. The underside can be coated with melted chocolate, like a Florentine, if desired.

Meringues

2 egg whites
110 g/4 oz castor or icing sugar, sifted, or use a mixture of
sugar (see method)

Whisk the egg whites until stiff, but not over-dry and crumbly. Castor sugar makes a less crisp meringue than all icing sugar. Whisk all the sugar gradually into the whisked egg whites or whisk in half the sugar and fold in the remainder; use a low speed with an electric mixer.

Lightly oil silicone baking trays or greaseproof paper on ordinary trays or use silicone (non-stick) paper. Either pipe small shapes of meringue (with a 5-mm/$\frac{1}{4}$-in pipe) or make rounds of about 2.5 cm/1 in with a teaspoon on to the paper or oiled trays. The quantities given make about 60 meringues.

Bake on the coolest oven setting (90-110 c, 200-225 F, gas 0-$\frac{1}{4}$) for 1-1$\frac{1}{4}$ hours. Cool then pack in airtight containers.

VARIATIONS

Italian Meringue: this technique of sweet-making gives a crisp meringue that is soft and chewy in the centre. Put 110 g/4 oz castor sugar and 4 tablespoons water into a strong saucepan; stir over a low heat until the sugar has dissolved. Boil to 'firm ball' stage or 121-127 c/250-260 F (the higher the temperature the crisper the meringues). Whisk the egg whites until stiff, gradually add the hot sugar mixture, whisking all the time until cold. Shape and bake as above.

Flavoured Meringue: add a few drops of vanilla essence (or use vanilla flavoured sugar) or other essences, such as ratafia or rum, to the whisked egg whites.

Chocolate Meringues: blend 25 g/1 oz chocolate powder with the sugar. Top the cooled cooked meringues with melted chocolate.

Coffee Meringues: blend 1-1$\frac{1}{2}$ teaspoons instant coffee powder with the sugar. Top the cooled cooked meringues with Glacé Icing (see page 107).

Nut Meringues: blend 50 g/2 oz very finely chopped hazelnuts or other nuts, or desiccated coconut, with the sugar.

Ratafias

2 egg whites
few drops almond or ratafia essence
150 g/5 oz ground almonds
150-175 g/5-6 oz castor sugar

Whisk the egg whites until frothy, do not over-beat. Mix in the remaining ingredients. Brush flat baking trays with a very little melted butter or oil. Form the mixture into about 60 tiny balls, put on to the trays. Bake for 10 minutes in the centre of a moderate oven (180 c, 350 f, gas 4). Cool slightly, remove from the baking trays on to a wire cooling tray. Use in trifles or as a petit-four.

VARIATIONS

Almond Macaroons: put the tiny balls on to rice paper. Bake as above. If you like them to be slightly sticky, place a bowl of water in the oven before baking. The small balls can be decorated with a piece of blanched almond or glacé cherry before cooking, or with melted chocolate when cold.

Chocolate Macaroons: follow the method of cooking Almond Macaroons but use 75 g/3 oz ground almonds, 25 g/1 oz cornflour and 50 g/2 oz chocolate powder to 150 g/5 oz castor sugar.

Coconut Macaroons: use half ground almonds and half desiccated coconut. Place the small balls on to rice paper, top with a piece of glacé cherry and bake as Ratafias.

YIELD OF SWEETMEATS

It is quite simple to ascertain the total amount that can be made from each recipe; simply add together the solid ingredients, such as sugar, dried fruit, butter, etc.

The number of sweetmeats that can be obtained from each recipe depends upon how large you wish these to be; a usual size is about 1.5-2.5-cm/$\frac{3}{4}$-1-in square if the mixture is placed in the size of tin recommended in the recipe.

Caramelled Fruits

Do not overlook the appeal of caramelled fresh fruit as part of a selection of petits-fours. The contrast between the sweet crisp coating and the juicy fresh flavour of the fruit is particularly appealing at the end of a meal.

The drawback of course about this method of preparing fruits is that they must be eaten the same day, unlike crystallized fruits, where the long immersion in sugar syrup preserves the fruit and turns it into a true sweetmeat.

The most suitable fruits to coat in caramel are grapes, (choose good-sized firm fruit) and tangerines (choose the seedless variety if possible).

150-175 g/5-6 oz grapes or tangerines
150 g/5 oz castor sugar
5 tablespoons water

Carefully remove the grapes from the stalks. Unless you particularly dislike the pips it is better not to remove these, for this allows the juice to seep into the caramel. If you do want to take out the pips, insert the tip of a small sharp knife and pull out the pips without making too large a cut in the fruit. Peel the tangerines, scrape off any white pith and divide the fruit into segments; do not remove the thin skin, this protects the juicy fruit. Should there be an odd pip remove this carefully.

Put the sugar and water into a strong saucepan, stir over a low heat until the sugar has dissolved then allow to boil, without stirring, until the mixture becomes a pale caramel, approximately 171 c/340 f.

Drop the fruit into the syrup, turn carefully with two metal spoons until each piece is coated thinly but evenly; take care not to crush the fruit in doing this.

Lift out and place on to a flat tin; there is no need to oil this. Leave until cold and hard and then place into small petits-fours paper cases.

Note If time does not allow to prepare these, see Frosted Fruits on page 106.

CHAPTER 7

PACKING SWEETMEATS

Throughout this book emphasis has been given to the importance of wrapping sweets and correct storage. There will be many occasions when you will be presenting homemade sweets as a gift, or making them to raise money for charity at a fête or bazaar. The appearance of the sweetmeats is then of great importance.

WRAPPING PAPERS

Waxed paper is recommended in many recipes, for it is pliable and easy to fold around the sweets and it keeps them in good condition. It is, however, not particularly attractive in appearance, and there are several other types of paper that could be used. These are obtainable from a good store or from stationers who specialise in cake and sweet containers.

You can obtain 'gold' and 'silver' wrapping paper; check when buying this that it is of the type suitable for contact with food; if doubtful, wrap the sweets first in waxed paper then in the metallic paper. You can buy coloured transparent-type paper, similar in texture to waxed paper, and fine Japanese wrapping papers. To wrap sweets, cut neat squares or rounds; practise folding the paper around the sweetmeat. Always have the joins on the base of the sweets.

CASES FOR SWEETMEATS

Small paper cases (often called confectionery or petits-fours cases) are sold in packets, either plain white, or with delicate patterns or in gold or silver. The cases not only look attractive, but they help to support rather fragile sweetmeats, such as fudge and truffles. The appearance of all sweetmeats and petits-fours is enhanced by being in the cases; these also make it easier to hold a sweetmeat or petit-four.

LINING PAPER

Containers for sweetmeats often need a lining paper. If you have a selection of different kinds of sweet, plain white or pale coloured paper looks attractive. You could use large doilies or baking parchment (which is firm enough to cut neatly). Aluminium foil also makes a good lining for containers.

CONTAINERS FOR SWEETS

If you are presenting sweets and/or petits-fours as a present, there are many containers that can be used. The most obvious is to pack the sweets in boxes, but you may wish to add to the value of the present by using something of greater value. People who collect interesting kitchen ware would be delighted to have a French type of flan dish filled with sweetmeats. Arrange these carefully, cover the whole container with cling film, then top with ribbon.

Small casseroles or other dishes could be filled in a similar way. Kitchen storage jars can also be filled with sweetmeats; if you are giving a set of jars you could fill each jar with a different kind of sweetmeat.

FILLING BOXES

Gift boxes are sold in stores and in many stationers. It is a good idea to buy the box or boxes before cutting the sweetmeats into squares or other shapes. You will then know exactly how they will fit, for a box looks much more attractive if it is well-filled, but not over-crowded. Fairly large shallow boxes enable you to display more sweetmeats. If using boxes that have already contained chocolates or sweets, cover them with gold, silver or patterned wrapping paper.

First line the base and sides of the box, see opposite; the lining paper should be sufficiently deep to form a cover over the top of the sweetmeats when the box is full. Arrange the sweets in the box. If you have a limited selection of two or three kinds of sweetmeat, then they can be arranged as in commercial boxes, with a good distribution of shape, size and coloured wrappings. It is a sensible idea to have a neat card inside detailing the various kinds of sweets and their position in the box. If you plan more than one layer of sweets, it is important to protect the first layer with a thick sheet of paper (or thin card covered with lining paper).

Top the filled boxes with ribbon.

Questions and Answers

Q. How does one prevent a sweet mixture crystallizing?
A. By stirring only as necessary; by brushing the inside of the pan with cold water to prevent the sweet mixture bubbling up the sides, drying out and crystallizing; by including cream of tartar or glucose in recipes where indicated; by not cooking too slowly.

Q. Why does the mixture for sweets sometimes burn?
A. Too thin a saucepan, or a pan with an uneven base; too little stirring (rich mixtures containing cream and butter must be stirred from time to time), and all sweetmeat mixtures should be stirred until the sugar has dissolved.

Q. Why does a sweetmeat not set properly?
A. It could be because an incorrect balance of ingredients was used, but it is more likely to be that the mixture was not cooked to the right stage or temperature, see pages 16 and 17. Often people stir the mixture so much that they prevent it ever reaching the right stage. If the sweetmeat has not set properly, tip it back into the saucepan, stir until melted again and try once more. Very damp weather can hinder setting.

Q. Why do toffees and other sweets, which are beautifully firm when first cooked, become soft and sticky after a short time?
A. This is due to exposure to the air and the natural humidity of the atmosphere. Wrap sweetmeats where advised. Store all sweetmeats in an airtight container, see page 12.

Q. Can one make sweets in a microwave cooker?
A. Yes, but there are certain points to consider:
a) you cannot use a metal saucepan; an ordinary ovenproof mixing bowl, which is excellent for many cooking purposes, may not withstand the intense heat to which many sugar mixtures have to be raised in order to set. Choose a flameproof container.
b) Mixtures must be stirred, where indicated in the recipe; this means opening the cooker door quite often.
c) Evaporation of liquid does not take place in a microwave cooker as readily as in a saucepan, so the saving of time may not be as great as anticipated.

Index